McDonald & Woodward 970.1
M
Indians Mounds of the
Atlantic Coast
30606

DATE DUE

DEC 4, 2003	

ST

PRINTED IN U.S.A.

INDIAN MOUNDS
OF THE ATLANTIC COAST

A Guide to Sites from Maine to Florida

Jerry N. McDonald

and

Susan L. Woodward

The McDonald & Woodward Publishing Company
Newark, Ohio
1987

The McDonald & Woodward Publishing Company
Guides to the American Landscape

INDIAN MOUNDS OF THE ATLANTIC COAST
A Guide to Sites from Maine to Florida

Copyright © 1987 by The McDonald & Woodward Publishing Company, P. O. Box 4098, Newark, Ohio 43055-8098
Library of Congress Catalog Number: 87-90428
ISBN 0-939923-03-3
Printed in the United States of America
by Lawhead Press, Inc., Athens, Ohio

A WORD TO USERS OF THIS BOOK

This book is a guide to the extant, publicly accessible prehistoric mounds and mound-like features of the Atlantic Coast Region; it is one of five guides that collectively will identify publicly accessible mound sites throughout Anglo-America. The **Atlantic Coast Region**, for purposes of this book, includes all or parts of each of the United States that borders the Atlantic Ocean, as well as parts of Vermont and West Virginia (Figure 1). Section I of this book provides an overview of selected geographical, chronological, and cultural characteristics of the various Indian groups that constructed mounds and mound-like features in the Atlantic Coast Region. Section I also reviews some of the ways in which mounds have been perceived during the 400 years since European settlement began in this region. Section II identifies and describes forty two extant, publicly accessible mounds and mound-like features located in the Atlantic Coast Region. Sources of additional information about this subject — Publications, Museums, and Topographic Maps — are identified in Section III.

The primary purpose of this book is to facilitate access by the interested public to information about Indian mounds and other prehistoric structures of the Atlantic Coast Region. We especially hope that this book will help people become aware of, visit, experience, and learn more about these features. We see this as a versatile publication, being of use to people with different interests in the archeological heritage of eastern North America — travelers, educators, students, archeologists, naturalists, recreation leaders, librarians, planners, and anybody else with a curious mind and an interest in seeing, understanding, and preserving the remaining record of North American prehistory.

ACKNOWLEDGMENTS

Many people throughout the eastern United States have generously helped assemble and evaluate information used in this book, and we sincerely thank each of them for their assistance. In particular, however, we would like to acknowledge the assistance of the following people who were extraordinarily helpful in providing us with detailed information about multiple sites: Douglas Bailey (West Virginia Office of Historic Preservation), Henry Baker (Florida Division of Historical Resources), Stanley Bond (Historic St. Augustine Preservation Board), Robert S. Carr (Dade County Historic Preservation Division), Michael Foley (South Carolina Department of Parks, Recreation and Tourism), David J. Hally (Department of Anthropology, University of Georgia), Patrick Romano (Pinellas County Park Department), Walter J. Rothenbach, Jr. (Sarasota County Parks and Recreation Department), John Scafidi (Florida Division of Recreation and Parks), John F. Scarry (Florida Division of Historical Resources), Marion Smith (Florida Division of Historical Resources), Arthur E. Spiess (Maine Historic Preservation Commission), Barbara Van Voast (Loxahatchee Historical Society), and Mark Williams (Department of Anthropology, University of Georgia). Assistance in obtaining photographs was generously provided by Eugene B. Barfield (Department of Anthropology, Indiana University), Carroll Dinsmore, Jr. (The Pictorial Studio, Damariscotta, Maine), Alan Marsh (National Park Service, Ocmulgee National Monument), Anna Peale (Indian Temple Mound Museum), Arthur E. Spiess (Maine Historic Preservation Commission), and Jim Weidhaas (Jekyll Island Authority). Cornelia Bailey and William Banks, Jr., were especially helpful in facilitating our access to the Sapelo Shell Ring. Arthur E. Spiess (Maine Historic Preservation Commission), Louis Tesar (Florida Division of Historical Resources), and Mark Williams (Department of Anthropology, University of Georgia) read and provided critical comments about an earlier draft of the manuscript for this book. We thank all of the above for helping to make this a better publication.

CONTENTS

INDIAN MOUNDS OF THE ATLANTIC COAST REGION

Mounds and mound-like features constitute the most conspicuous record of prehistoric human activity remaining on the landscape of eastern North America. These raised earthen, stone and shell artifacts — present in many different forms, sizes, levels of complexity and concentration — document at least 7,000 years of eastern North American prehistory. In the **Atlantic Coast Region** (Figure 1), American Indians built a great variety of mounds and mound-like features over at least the last 5,000 years of prehistory (older features are found north and west of the region in eastern Canada and the Mississippi Valley). Thousands of shell middens, including some of the largest such middens in Anglo-America, were built along the Atlantic and Gulf coasts and many of the rivers of this region. Some of the earliest, most complex, and unusual mounds, earthworks, and associated landscape alterations to be found anywhere in Anglo-America were constructed in Florida. The concept of elaborate ceremonialism that often involved use of earthen mounds and earthworks also spread east, northeast, and southeast from the great mound building centers in the middle Ohio and middle Mississippi valleys into the Atlantic Coast Region. As a result, earthen conical mounds and earthworks were built from New York to Florida during the Woodland Period; later, primarily during the Mississippian Period, earthen platform mounds were raised from North Carolina to Florida. Stone mounds and other, often enigmatic, stone features were constructed from New York to Florida.

Unfortunately, most of the mounds and mound-like features that were present in the Atlantic Coast Region and elsewhere in eastern North America four hundred years ago when European settlement of the region began either have been destroyed or altered to the extent that they cannot now be easily recognized. The destruction or alteration of these features has occurred as a result of the transformation of eastern North America into agricultural, transportation and urban landscapes by people primarily of European origin. A small number of mounds and mound-like features, however, have survived. These remaining features provide modern observers with an opportunity to experience, first hand, physical expressions of lifeways and cultural values that are at once gone but inescapably part of the cultural legacy of eastern North America.

1

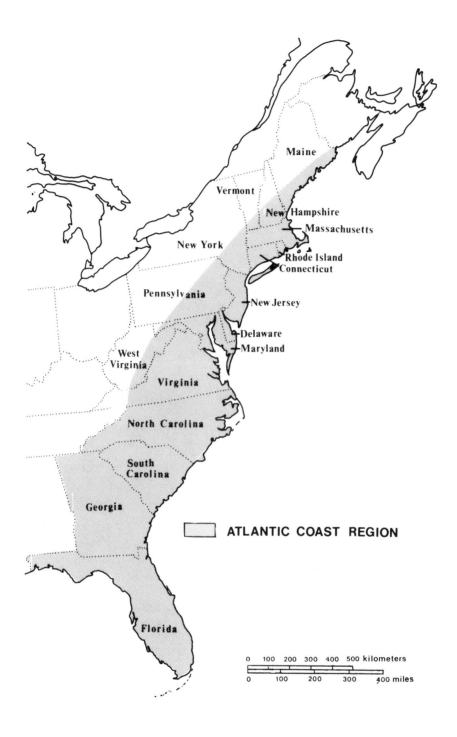

Figure 1. The Atlantic Coast Region, as defined in this book.

2

SECTION I

MOUNDS AND RELATED FEATURES OF THE ATLANTIC COAST REGION: ARCHEOLOGICAL AND HISTORICAL CONTEXT

MOUNDS AND RELATED FEATURES IN ARCHEOLOGICAL CONTEXT

The mounds and mound-like features of the Atlantic Coast Region were built by many groups of Indians for several different reasons over a span of 5,000 or more years. Basically, two categories of prehistoric architectural structures are represented in the Atlantic Coast Region — (1) shell middens and (2) mounds, earthworks and related features. Each category derived from a different process. Shell middens resulted from the accumulation of shell from shellfish, and other waste, at habitation or exploitation sites. Mounds, earthworks, and related features were constructed to serve some specific function(s). Sometimes the two processes were combined such that midden debris was deliberately formed into mounds, causeways, or other functional structures. Shellfishing and mound building among prehistoric people are much older than the earliest dated remains of these activities in the Atlantic Coast Region, and it is quite possible that older evidence of such activities awaits discovery in the region.

Shell middens began to be formed over large parts of the Atlantic Coast Region by at least a few centuries before 5,000 years ago (e.g., Turner Farm Site, Maine; St. Johns River sites, Florida) and continued to be formed into the Historic Period (e.g., Fort Shantok, Connecticut; Mound Key, Florida). Mound and earthwork construction appeared in this region around 3,000 years ago — perhaps developing out of several nuclei such as Belle Glade I in southern Florida, or more likely from the Adena and Ohio Hopewell in the middle Ohio Valley. Like middens, mounds and earthworks were constructed into the Historic Period, but — in the Atlantic Coast area — primarily only in the southern part of the region. Midden formation was a usual by-product of an ecological process carried out wherever conditions permitted in the Atlantic Coast Region. The use of mounds and earthworks in this region, however, was largely based on ideas introduced from outside the Atlantic Coast area (e.g., the Ohio and Mississippi valleys, or Mesoamerica) and the popularity of the practice tended to wax and wane in synchrony with the rise and fall of influence from those source regions.

The increase in midden formation after 5,000 years ago may be attributed to several factors, including (1) human population growth, (2) increased specialization in the collecting of shellfish, and (3) environmental changes that allowed increased shellfish productivity. Middens probably were formed before 5,000 years ago in the Atlantic Coast Region, but these would have been generally smaller than the later middens and are more likely to have been destroyed or obscured by erosion, sedimentation, or inundation. Mound and earthwork construction was related in relatively complex ways to (1) human population growth, (2) increased sedentism (the tendency to remain settled in one area for longer periods of time), (3) increased social organization and class or role distinctions, (4) increased social and political stability, (5) increased ceremonialism (especially mortuary ceremonialism), and (6) new adaptations for environmental exploitation (e.g., house mounds or raised fields in areas with high water tables).

PREHISTORIC ENVIRONMENTS OF THE ATLANTIC COAST REGION

The Atlantic Coast Region, spanning almost 24° of latitude and ranging from sea level to nearly 7,000' above sea level, comprises a great variety of local environments today, as it did at the time of earliest European contacts around 400-500 years ago. These environments provided a wide variety of resources to the prehistoric Indian inhabitants of the region, and — in that variety — had stimulated different adaptations to regional conditions by the various Indian groups. The environments of the Atlantic Coast Region 12,000 years ago, however, near the end of the last glacial period, were considerably less diverse than during the late prehistoric period. The Indian inhabitants of that earlier time had a more uniform way of life throughout the entire region than those of later times. Several significant environmental changes of the last 12,000 years influenced how, where, and to what extent Indians of eastern North America used resources and territories. These included regional warming and increased precipitation, and the influence of such changes on deglaciation, sea level and coastline stability, stream characteristics (water volume, turbidity, seasonal flow patterns), and the composition and distribution of biotic (plant and animal) communities.

The Atlantic Coast Region is composed of parts of two physiographic (landform) provinces, the Atlantic-Gulf Coastal Plain and the Appalachian Highlands (Figure 2). That part of the Atlantic-Gulf Coastal Plain that is above sea level extends from Cape Cod, Massachusetts, south to Florida, then west through Texas into Mexico. The width of this part of the province varies, only touching the coast along parts of southern New England but increasing to about 200 miles in width in Georgia. All of Florida is included in this province. The part of this province that is below sea level — the Continental Shelf — extends east and south from the present coastline for distances up to 200 miles off Florida and Massachusetts. The Continental Shelf is bounded seaward by the Continental Slope, the edge of the continent that drops off rapidly to greater depths (Figure 2). Most of the Coastal Plain is composed of loose or poorly consolidated clays, sands, gravels,

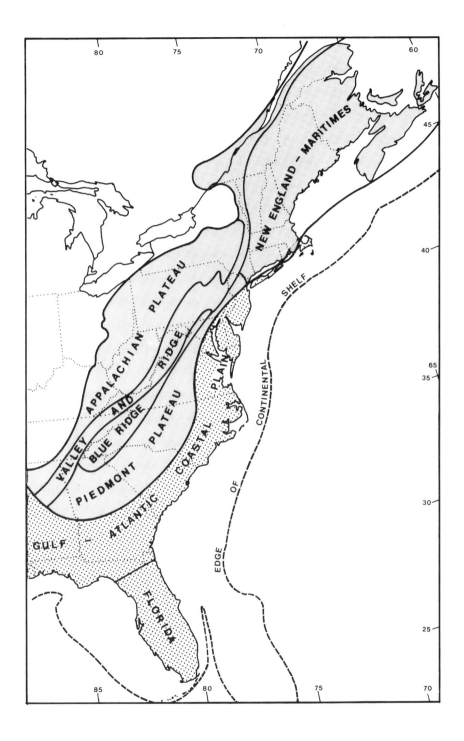

Figure 2. The physiographic regions of eastern North America.

and marls. Much of Florida, a distinct section of the Coastal Plain, consists largely of raised beds of marine limestone and coral, and contains many lakes. Typically, the coastline of the Coastal Plain is characterized by drowned valleys, shallow embayments, and barrier islands backed by lagoons and marshes.

The Appalachian Highlands lie north and west of the Coastal Plain, and are oriented in a northeast-southwest direction. The northern end of this province, the New England-Maritime section, has been scraped and sculpted several times during the Quaternary (the current Ice Age) by continental glaciers. The largely metamorphic bedrock is covered with a thin veneer of glacial debris or marine clays. Lakes dot the interior, while long arms of the sea reach inland via the numerous island-strewn bays. The Piedmont section is a land of generally low elevations, rolling hilly surfaces, and deeply weathered soils. The Blue Ridge, reaching to almost 6,700′, comprises the highest elevations in the Appalachian Highlands. The northern Blue Ridge and the Valley and Ridge consist largely of narrow northeast-southwest trending ridges paralleled by intervening elongate valleys. The surface of the southern Blue Ridge is more irregular, varying from rolling hills to high ridges and mountain peaks. West of the Valley and Ridge is the Appalachian Plateau, the westernmost section of the Appalachian Highlands. This is an area of level uplands incised by numerous streams, most of which are tributary to the Ohio River. The Appalachian Plateau slopes generally to the west, with elevations varying from about 4,800′ to 1,200′ above sea level. Soils are thin on the slopes and upland surfaces of the New England-Maritime, Blue Ridge, Valley and Ridge, and Appalachian Plateau sections, whereas some of the valleys contain appreciably greater amounts of colluvial and alluvial soils. Generally thin or poor soils, combined with the comparatively high elevations or latitudes of these sections, made them relatively unsuitable for horticulture during the prehistoric period.

Many rivers occur in the Atlantic Coast Region, and almost without exception these flow radially away from the Appalachian Highlands toward the Atlantic Ocean or Gulf of Mexico. North of New Jersey, these streams cross only the Appalachian Highlands before reaching the sea, but from southern New Jersey through western Florida they also cross the Coastal Plain. Such rivers form natural routes connecting coastal areas with those of the interior and, along their course, typically pass through a variety of different habitats. Deep deposits of alluvium form the floodplain of the larger, low gradient streams where they cross the Piedmont and Coastal Plain. These alluvial floodplains represented the most productive sites for prehistoric horticulture in the Atlantic Coast Region. The St. Johns River, Florida, one of the few large rivers in the Atlantic region that does not drain from the Appalachian Highlands, is an unusual string of alternating lakes and broad, slow-moving stream segments that finally reaches the sea via a long, narrow drowned valley. This highly productive stream system was exploited extensively by Florida Indians.

As is to be expected for a region with such a large latitudinal extent, climate over the area varies greatly. Average annual precipitation ranges from about 60″ in Florida to about 45″ in Maine. Most precipitation comes during the summer months and is adequate to support forest vegetation throughout the region. Temperatures also vary considerably throughout the region, with those of the southern part being significantly higher than those of the northern part. The southern part of the Atlantic Coast Region has a growing season more than twice as long as the northern part, an important environmental pattern that strongly influenced the biological productivity of different regions and the spread of prehistoric horticulture.

At the time of European contact, forests dominated the vegetation of the Atlantic Coast Region. There was, however, considerable variation in the composition of these forests — and in the animal life associated with them — in different parts of the region. In the northern part of the Atlantic Coast Region, conifers such as hemlock and white pine were either the dominant species or they codominated with such deciduous broadleaf species as American beech, sugar maple, or northern red oak. The short growing season and the relatively low carrying capacity of the conifer or mixed forests resulted in generally less animal biomass (total animals, by weight) than was typical in areas farther south. Bear, white-tailed deer, elk and moose were economically important large terrestrial mammals, while seals and whales were important among the marine resources accessible to Indians of the area. From southern New England and New York south to Florida was the Temperate Deciduous Forest, a mosaic of several different forest communities unified by the fact that the dominant species were deciduous. The Temperate Deciduous Forest of the Atlantic Coast Region was dominated by several species of oak, hickory, and chestnut which, along with walnut and beech, provided an abundant supply of nutritious food for many animals, including humans. Turkey and white-tailed deer were most important among the larger game animals of the region. Considerable local variation in the forests of the Atlantic Coast Region occurred because of differences in slope, elevation, soil characteristics, ground water level, precipitation, fire history, and other factors — including disturbances caused by humans. Over most of the Atlantic Coast Region, however, the forests — the plants and their animal associates — provided abundant and diverse biotic resources for use by Indians.

When the last continental glacier began to recede 18,000 years ago, the northern part of the Atlantic Coast Region was covered by glacial ice. Compared to present conditions, sea level was 400′-600′ lower, the unglaciated part of the Coastal Plain was much wider, temperatures and precipitation levels were lower, growing seasons were shorter, forests were less diverse and were more frequently dominated by conifer species, the large-bodied mammal community was much more diverse, and shellfish productivity was lower. The warming trend accompanying the transition from glacial to interglacial conditions had produced some environmental changes — such

9

as partial deglaciation and initiation of rising sea levels — by the beginning of the Paleo-Indian Period, about 12,000 years ago. The environment available to the Paleo-Indians, however, was still relatively uniform and less productive biologically than it would become by around 7,000-5,000 years ago. By about 5,000 years ago, stream regimes, rising sea level, and differentiation of biotic communities in eastern North America had become fairly well stabilized, signaling the development of relative equilibrium among the various major physical and biological processes operating in the region. For our purposes, two aspects of this environmental stabilization are especially important: (1) the slowing of sea level rise and the development of slower flowing streams containing warmer, clearer water created improved habitats for shellfish, and (2) the presence of diverse, productive, relatively stable terrestrial environments provided greater environmental security to Indian groups. This latter condition contributed to different ecological specialization, population growth, expanded interregional trade, and social change among these Indian groups. Shell midden formation and mound-and-earthwork construction were, respectively, direct and indirect results of the human exploitation of, and adaptation to, the new diverse, productive Holocene (the current interglacial) environments.

INCREASING SHELLFISH PRODUCTIVITY AND THE APPERANCE OF SHELL MIDDENS

Sea level has been rising along the coasts of the world during the last 18,000-16,000 years as a result of the melting of the glaciers that covered large parts of the northern hemisphere during the last glaciation. The rate and extent of sea level rise has varied locally according to differences in the flexibility and buoyancy behavior of the continents as a result of different unloading (deglaciation or erosion) or loading (sedimentation or increasing water load) patterns. Generally, the Atlantic and Gulf coasts of Anglo-America experienced a relatively rapid rise of sea level between 15,000-5,000 years ago, with a slower rise over the last 5,000 years. Coastal areas of New England and the Canadian Maritime Provinces have actually undergone two significant periods of rising sea level during the last 18,000 years — the last beginning around 9,000 years ago and slowing around 3,000 years ago. Along the middle Atlantic and Gulf coasts, the rate of rise began to slow, at different places, between 7,000 and 3,000 years ago. Sea level is still rising along the Atlantic Coast Region at a generally slow but not uniform rate. For example, the rate along the northeast coast of Maine is 1' each 100 years while at places on the Gulf Coast of Florida the rate is between 2"-4" each 100 years. Changes in the circulation of waters in the North Atlantic Ocean have accompanied the rise in sea level and have resulted in warmer water being transported farther north along the southeast coast of the United States. This warming contributed to improved conditions for the growth of many species of shellfish along much of the Atlantic Coast.

The changes in sea level along the Atlantic and Gulf coasts have influenced how and where Indians utilized coastal environments and their resources. Shellfish collecting at coastal sites probably took place from the time that humans first entered the region but it is probable that this activity increased in frequency, intensity, and significance only after the rate of sea level rise slowed. The slowed rise permitted the accumulation of mud and sand deposits along the coast, which contributed to the development of marsh, barrier island-and-lagoon, and shallow drowned river valley ecosystems in which some species of shellfish were very productive. Indians of the Middle Archaic Period and after exploited these productive ecosystems intensively. With the intensified exploitation of, and increased dependence upon, shellfish resources during the Middle Archaic Period, piles of shell debris began to accumulate at exploitation and habitation sites.

Just as changes in sea level influenced the location and productivity of shellfish resources, so did changes in regional temperature, precipitation, and erosion influence the location and productivity of shellfish resources in rivers and lakes. Regional warming associated with deglaciation contributed in several ways to improve shellfish habitat in inland waters. The melting of glaciers initially caused high water and sediment levels in many river systems, but as the glaciers disappeared water flow and sediment levels were reduced. Vegetation growth in deglaciated areas, enhanced by warming temperatures, further stabilized loose sediments and contributed to clearer waters. Water temperature increased. Over parts of eastern North America, including the southern part of the Atlantic Coast Region, precipitation was lower than at present for prolonged periods and stream flow was reduced accordingly. These environmental conditions contributed to an increase in shellfish productivity in inland locations which, in turn, was accompanied by an intensified exploitation of the shellfish by Middle Archaic peoples and those that followed. As along the coasts, shell middens began to form at exploitation sites along rivers and lakes and continued to be formed or enlarged into the Historic Period.

A CHRONOLOGICAL AND CULTURAL OUTLINE OF THE MOUND BUILDING INDIANS OF THE ATLANTIC COAST REGION

The human prehistory of North America has been divided into various units of time and culture by archeologists. Here, we follow the practice of referring to units of time as **Periods**, and units of culture as **Traditions** or **Phases** (Figure 3). Each Period represents a span of time during which (theoretically) certain general cultural characteristics were well established and widely distributed among populations of American Indians. The sets of general cultural characteristics shared by dispersed populations of Indians are called Traditions. Phases are more specific, localized, and complexly-defined cultural units within a Tradition (Table 1).

North America has been populated by humans for at least 12,000 years, and possibly longer. The last 12,000 years of human prehistory in the eastern United States and adjacent parts of Canada — the Eastern Woodlands

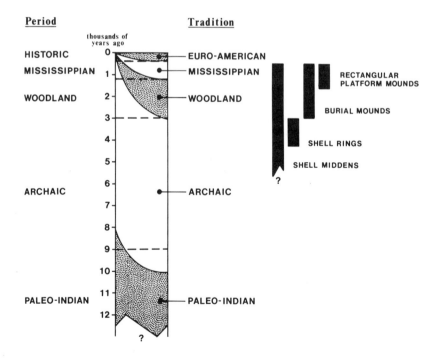

Figure 3. The general chronology of North American prehistory and midden and mound building activity in the Atlantic Coast Region. Broken horizontal lines indicate the approximate boundaries of **Periods.** The approximate duration of **Traditions** is shown by alternating stippled and open fields. All time lines are arbitrary and suggestive only.

Table 1: Culture Phases Mentioned in Text

	Phase	Location	Approximate Duration*
I	Archaic Tradition		
	Poverty Point	Northern Louisiana	1000-700 BC
	St. Simons -Orange	Coastal South Carolina - Northern Florida	2500-500 BC
II	Woodland Tradition		
	Adena	Middle Ohio Valley	1000 BC-AD 100
	Belle Glade	Lake Okeechobee Basin	500 BC-Contact
	Deptford	Coastal South Carolina - Gulf Coast of Florida	500 BC-AD 600
	Ohio Hopewell	Middle Ohio Valley	150 BC-AD 500
	Havana Hopewellian	Illinois and Northern Middle Mississippi Valleys	150 BC-AD 500
	Copena Hopewellian	Middle Tennessee Valley	150 BC-AD 500
	Santa Rosa - Swift Creek	Southern Georgia - Southeastern Alabama - Western Florida	AD 1-AD 500
	St. Johns Complex	East and Central Florida	500 BC-Contact
	Weeden Island Complex	Western Florida - Southern Georgia	AD 300-1000
III	Mississippian Tradition		
	Middle Mississippi	Middle Mississippi Valley	AD 700-1200
	Macon Plateau	Central Georgia	AD 900-1100
	Lamar	Georgia	AD 1350-Contact
	Pee Dee	South Central North Carolina	AD 1400-1650
	Pisgah	Eastern Tennessee - Western North Carolina - Northern Georgia	AD 1100-1450
	Qualla	Eastern Tennessee - Western North Carolina - Northern Geogia	AD 1450-Contact
	Fort Walton	Western Florida	AD 1000-Contact
	Safety Harbor	Tampa Bay Region, Florida	AD 1400-Contact

*The dates given for the duration of all phases are approximate and do not necessarily apply throughout all parts of the geographic range of any given phase.

culture region — is divided into four Periods — Paleo-Indian, Archaic, Woodland, and Mississippian — with names corresponding to the four dominant Traditions of this region.

The Paleo-Indian Period includes the time from about 12,000-9,000 years ago and encompasses the earliest people known with certainty to have lived in eastern North America. The Paleo-Indian Tradition is characterized by the manufacture and use of finely worked lanceolate (leaf-shaped) projectile points and associated flaked stone tools, and the nomadic hunting of large game animals, many species of which became extinct during the Paleo-Indian Period. Paleo-Indians were, in fact, broad-based hunters and gatherers who were relatively mobile and culturally uniform over most of their cumulative range. Individual population units were small and exploitation territories were relatively large.

As many of the large-bodied mammal species (mastodonts, mammoths, horses, camels, and others) became extinct and other environmental changes transpired, human lifestyles changed, leading to what is now recognized as the Archaic Tradition. Initially, Indians of the Archaic Period were nomadic hunters, gatherers, fishers and collectors who traveled about in small groups and manufactured flaked stone tools. In many respects Early Archaic people were very similar to Paleo-Indians, perhaps the main differences being that they utilized a greater variety of plant and animal resources and exploited smaller territories. Through the Middle and Late parts of the Archaic Period, however, post-glacial environmental change progressed to the extent that many different and highly productive environments came to exist throughout the Eastern Woodlands. In response, Archaic peoples became ecologically diversified, establishing a basic pattern of regional cultural differences that changed in detail but, fundamentally, persisted into the Historic Period. Among the important cultural changes that occurred at this time were increased specialization in the exploitation of local resources, the widespread adoption of ground and polished stone tools, greater sedentism (tendency to remain settled in fewer locations for longer periods), and the formation of larger population units. Overall, the population of Archaic Indians was slowly increasing, and exploitation territories were becoming smaller or otherwise more intensively utilized. It was during the Middle Archaic Period that conspicuous enduring material landscape features were first produced in eastern North America: **shell middens** began to be formed as a result of the increased exploitation of shellfish resources and small **burial mounds** appeared along the coast of Quebec and Labrador as monuments reflecting the increasingly material expression of mortuary (death and burial) ceremonialism. Shell middens dating from the Middle Archaic Period are known from the Atlantic Coast Region, but mound construction is not known to have taken place in the Atlantic states until around 3,000 years ago.

Toward the end of the Archaic Period, four other significant cultural characteristics appeared in the Eastern Woodlands: the manufacture of fiber tempered ceramic pottery, the development of interregional trade networks, the practice of horticulture, and burial of the dead in mounds (the Middle Archaic Period burial mounds from Labrador are north of the Eastern Woodlands Region). When fully developed, these four practices, along with the development of semi-permanent and permanent villages and tribal-size social groups, characterized the Woodland Tradition.

The Woodland Period began about 3,000-2,500 years ago. Woodland people were primarily hunters, fishers, gatherers, or collectors; they intensively utilized various resources within their exploitation territories. Tool technology was based on flaked and ground stone, bone, and wood; clay ceramics were tempered with sand, ground stone, or shell. Horticulture was present among some Woodland populations from the earliest appearance of the Tradition, but was not present or economically important in many groups until into the Late Woodland Period. The regional population continued to increase. This increased the stress on resources within exploitation territories; greater specialization in resource acquisition and distribution became necessary. Some adjustments to the growing pressure included the development of more efficient and cooperative forms of social organization, the establishment of semi-permanent or permanent settlement centers, and the formation of more extensive and formally regulated trade networks (Figure 4). Clearly ranked societies with distinct status differences appeared. The Woodland Tradition reached its overall cultural climax during the Middle Woodland Period, when interregional trade, cultural complexity, and the accumulation of individual wealth seem to have been at their peak. The Ohio, Havana (Illinois-Iowa-Missouri), and Copena (Alabama-Tennessee) Hopewell(ian) phases apparently were the major focal points of this cultural climax; the region integrated and affected by trade and information flow during this time is called the Hopewell Interaction Sphere. The Atlantic Coast Region was an integral part of the Hopewell Interaction Sphere, providing and receiving durable exotic raw materials as well as cultural concepts.

Mound building was present in parts of the Atlantic Coast Region from the earliest appearance of the Woodland Tradition. People of the Belle Glade I Phase of the Lake Okeechobee Basin, Florida, built house mounds as early as 2,500 years ago. Contact between Belle Glade people and others to the north could have resulted in the spread of the mound concept northward. Similarly burial mounds were being constructed on the north shore of the Gulf of St. Lawrence at this time, from which area the concept could have diffused southward. The most likely and important source of the mound building concept for most of the Atlantic Coast Region, however, appears to have been the middle Ohio Valley. The practice of mound building, especially the building of burial mounds and the use of associated elements of mortuary ceremonialism, took form in the middle Ohio Valley around 3,000-2,000 years ago and began to diffuse into the middle Atlantic Coast Region during the Early Woodland Period in conjunction with the

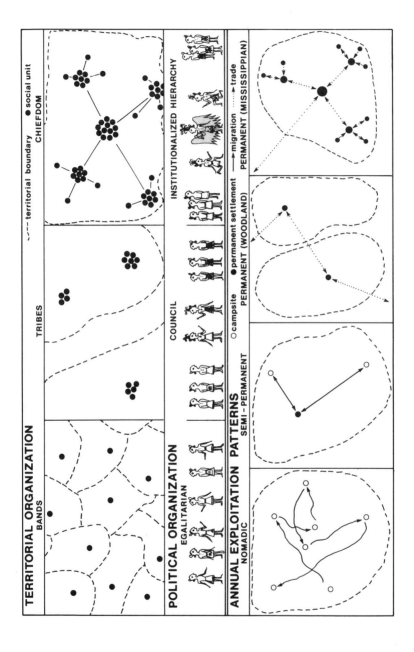

Figure 4. Generalized patterns of territorial and socio-political organization and of resource exploitation and exchange which developed among the Indians of the Atlantic Coast Region.

spread of Adena Phase influence. Woodland mortuary ceremonialism and burial mound use reached its peak during the Middle Woodland Period, a reflection of the influence of the Ohio Hopewell and on surrounding Indian cultures (Figure 5). During the Late Woodland Period, mound building regressed throughout much of the Atlantic Coast Region except in the southern part of that area. Indeed, the mound building Weeden Island Complex of southern Georgia, southeastern Alabama, and western Florida flourished and represents a rare example of a regional cultural climax during the Late Woodland Period. The construction of rectangular platform mounds in the Atlantic Coast Region might have originated among the Weeden Island people.

The construction of ceremonial earthworks was not widespread in the Atlantic Coast Region, being represented mainly in South Carolina, Georgia, and Florida. Earthen bases for village stockades were built in the middle Atlantic and southern New England areas.

About 1,200 years ago the Mississippian Tradition appeared in the Mississippi Valley and subsequently spread through much of the southeastern United States (Figure 6). The development of this Tradition rests upon several cultural elements that either derived from Mesoamerica (Figure 7; Table 2) or other unknown source areas, or developed locally. The Mississippian Tradition is characterized by great reliance on maize agriculture, the development of large permanent population clusters at — or affiliated with — permanent ceremonial centers, well developed social and political organization with an institutionalized hierarchy of offices of rank and power, the construction of platform mounds and adjacent public ceremonial spaces, the paraphernalia of the Southern Ceremonial Complex, and new ceramic designs. Hunting, fishing and collecting continued to be practiced (use of the bow and arrow reached the Eastern Woodlands by A.D. 400), but farming was an extremely important and often the dominant economic pursuit of Mississippian peoples. Consequently, most Mississippian settlements were closely associated with alluvial river valleys although some were located near lakes or the Gulf Coast. Central place (settlement) hierarchies often existed, with a dominant governing center controlling subordinate centers, which in turn dominated local hamlets or farmsteads. Symbols, objects, and costumes of the Southern Ceremonial Complex helped define rank and authority (Figure 8). During the Early Mississippian Period, about A.D. 900-1200, colonists from the Mississippi Valley diffused east as far as the Atlantic Coast Region. One postulated pathway of diffusion was via the Tennessee River Valley, then across the Piedmont, as far as central Georgia, while another was along the Gulf Coastal Plain as far as the southern Chattahoochee-Apalachicola River Valley and environs. These colonists established farming enclaves along productive alluvial river valleys amidst the resident Woodland Indians. By about 1,200 years ago, Mississippian and Woodland peoples living side by side had become acculturated to the extent that sharp differences between the two were blurred. This wide-

17

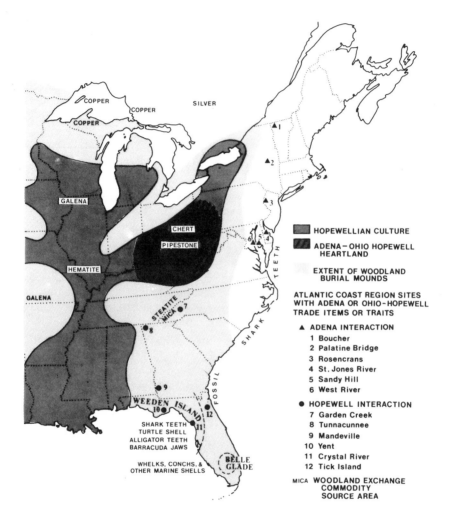

Figure 5. Generalized pattern of Woodland burial mound distribution and its relationship to the Woodland cultural climaxes and Woodland (Adena and Hopewell) Interaction Sphere. Representative souce areas for trade goods and eastern sites with Adena-Hopewellian traits are shown. Generally, evidence of Adena interaction is stronger in the northern half of the Atlantic Coast Region while that of Hopewell is stronger in the southern half. Some burial mounds occur northeast of the limits indicated here, but these are rare. (After Seemans, 1979 and Coe, Snow and Benson, 1986.)

18

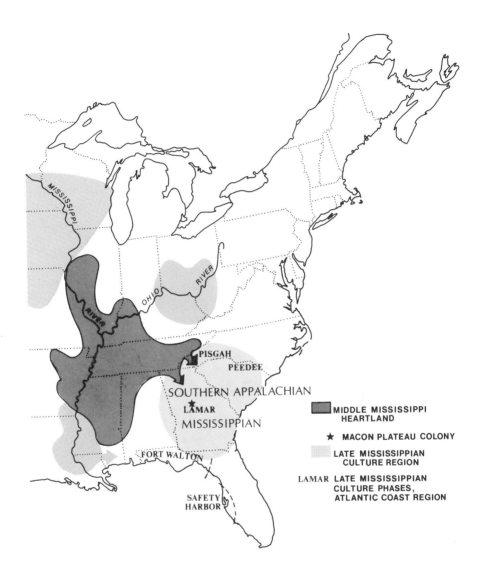

Figure 6. The Middle Mississippi (Early Mississippian) nucleus, postulated routes of diffusion southeastward from that cultural heartland, and Late Mississippian culture phases in the southeast. The Macon Plateau colony, remnants of which are preserved today as Ocmulgee National Monument, was an outlier of Middle Mississippi culture during the Early Mississippi Period.

spread acculturation created many regional variants within the general Mississippian culture sphere. The southeastern division of the Late Mississippian culture sphere has been called the Southern Appalachian Mississippian culture region; occurring in or near this Southern Appalachian region were such phases as Fort Walton, Safety Harbor, Pisgah, Pee Dee, and Lamar (Figure 6).

Mounds were integral and conspicuous parts of Mississippian settlements. One or more platform mounds, usually but not always built on a rectangular base and with one or more distinct ascending ramps, formed the centerpiece of Mississippian ceremonial centers. Temples, residences of leaders, or other structures used by the elite were located on these mounds. Public ceremonial space usually adjoined the mounds. When more than one platform mound was present — as was typical for larger ceremonial centers — they were usually of different sizes, implying that they might be physical indicators of the relative rank of activities that took place on or before them. Earthworks were sometimes constructed around or within these ceremonial centers. Although Mississippian people typically buried their dead in cemeteries, some burials were made in mounds. Deceased members of the political and religious elite were frequently buried in the ceremonial platform mounds, sometimes along with members of their family or their retainers. When a member of the elite died and was buried, the structures on his mound were often ritually burned. Later, the mound would be reconditioned, enlarged, and readied for its next occu-

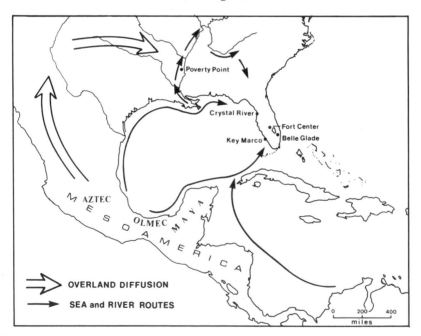

Figure 7. Hypothetical routes of diffusion of ideas and materials from Mesoamerica to southeastern North America. (See Table 2.)

Table 2: Some Cultural Elements of Known or Suspected Mesoamerican or South American Origin[1]

Major cultigens:

    Squash and pumpkins *(Cucurbita)*
    Gourds *(Lagenaria)*
    Maize *(Zea maize)*
    Beans *(Phaseolus)*

Ceramics:

    Fiber tempered pottery
    Effigy pottery (some styles)
    Tripod vessels

Catamarans

Stelae

Raised agricultural fields

Mounds:

    Rectangular platform mounds
    Custom of rebuilding and enlarging platform mounds

Ceremonial plaza adjoining platform mounds

Some elements of the Southern Ceremonial Complex

[1]Some people who have studied the development of Native American culture in eastern North America believe that many elements in this table could have developed independently in the region. This table is presented to identify elements used to support the concept of diffusion from Mesoamerica and South America into eastern North America, not to imply that diffusion was necessarily the only process by which these elements could have been acquired by Indians in the Atlantic Coast Region.

pant. Some conical and truncated rectangular mounds also were built specifically for mortuary ceremonialism and burials.

Mound construction and use was still being practiced in parts of the Atlantic Coast Region (as well as other areas to the west) when European colonization began. Mound use came to an end very soon after the Europeans arrived, however, largely because disease and warfare decimated many Indian populations, and European expansion caused the dislocation of remaining Indian settlements. The same is true for shell midden construction. Villages or exploitation sites were depopulated or the remaining Indians were displaced soon after European settlement began, and shell midden construction quickly came to an end.

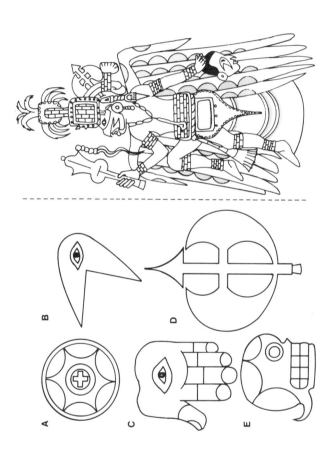

Figure 8. Symbols and costumes representative of the Southern Ceremonial Complex. A — Sun circle; B — Forked eye; C — Hand and eye; D — Bi-lobed arrow; E — Death's head. The costumed figure at right was compiled from figures on copper plates found at the Etowah Ceremonial Center. The variety of symbols, objects, and costumes associated with the Southern Ceremonial Complex was substantially greater than that presented in this figure.

MOUNDS AND SIMILAR STRUCTURES OF THE ATLANTIC COAST REGION

The Atlantic Coast Region contains a rich variety of mounds and mound-like features — including some of the rarest and most complex prehistoric public works to be found anywhere in Anglo-America (Figure 9). The list of artificial landscape features includes shell middens (including shell rings), shell mounds, stone mounds, stone walls, earthen mounds, earthworks, terraces, breakwaters, graded ways, sunken roads, canals, wells, and ponds — all resulting from the artificial manipulation of significant volumes of earth, stone or shell. The major types of features to be found in the Atlantic Coast Region are identified and briefly described below. The diversity of detail that actually exists among individual features within any category is, however, much more extensive than these general descriptions indicate.

Shell middens or **shell heaps** are piles of refuse that develop around habitation or exploitation sites; these are composed of high proportions of shell (Figure 10), usually mixed with other discarded cultural debris (pottery shards, bones, stone tools, ashes, charcoal, etc.). Middens vary considerably in size and form. Some are barely perceptible scatterings of a few shells, whereas others are quite large and reflect the deliberate concentration of great volumes of refuse over extended periods of time. Middens may be nearly level surface or subsurface features, or such distinct raised features as localized low piles, low mounds, high mounds, linear ridges, arcing or sinuous ridges, or somewhat amorphous combinations of these. Generally middens are larger in the south than in the north, reflecting the greater productivity of southern ecosystems and the absolutely greater use of shellfish by southern Indians. Between periods of use, non-cultural sediments sometimes accumulated on these middens, soils developed, and plant and animal life became established. Consequently middens consist of irregular patches and layers of cultural and noncultural materials.

Shell middens began to accumulate by at least 7,000 years ago during the Middle Archaic Period, and continued to be formed into the Historic Period. No single midden in eastern North America, of course, spans the entire 7,000 years; most cover only a very small part of that period and some conceivably represent the remains of only a single meal or feast. Inland middens located along streams and lakes usually are dominated by the remains of freshwater mussels of various species, although those along the St. Johns River in Florida are composed largely of pond snails (*Viviparous georgianus*). The composition of coastal middens varies. The shell in northern coastal middens is usually dominated by a single species — either soft shell clam (*Mya arenaria*), hard shell clam or quahog (*Mercenaria mercenaria*), or oyster (*Crassostrea virginica*) — depending upon latitude and local ecological conditions. The shell in southern middens often

SHELL MIDDEN
○ **SHELL RING**
▲ **CONICAL MOUND**
▲ **STONE MOUND**
▲ **PLATFORM MOUND**
⊏ **EARTHWORK**
★ **KEY DWELLER SITE**

ST. AUGUSTINE
MERIGOMISH HARBOR
OAK BAY
ST. MARGARET'S BAY
FRENCHMAN BAY
TURNER FARM SITE
NEW HARBOR
CROUCH'S COVE
WHEELER'S SITE
EAGLE HILL
ANDOVER
NORTON SITE
AURORA
PRUDENCE ISLAND
EAGLE HILL
CROTON-ON-HUDSON
PARKER SITE
SOUTH AMBOY
COTUIT
SQUIBNOCKET POND
OLD LYME
SHINNECOCK HILLS
PORT WASHINGTON
KAESAR SITE
CONASKONCK POINT
KENT COUNTY
POPES CREEK
WOLFE NECK
PICKAWAXENT CREEK
DON BOSCO SCHOOL
JEFFERSON'S MOUND
WOOD'S GAP
BRANDON SHELL MOUND
T. F. NELSON MOUND
ASHEVILLE
HARKERS ISLAND
PERMUDA ISLAND
PEACHTREE MOUND
CAMDEN
TUGALOO
REMBERT MOUNDS
STALLINGS ISLAND
HOLLYWOOD MOUND
STRATTON PLACE
FIG ISLAND
SKULL CREEK
LAMAR
IRENE MOUND
MANDEVILLE
ROOD CREEK
SAPELO ISLAND
CANNON POINT
JEKYLL ISLAND
LAKE MICCOSUKEE
CUMBERLAND ISLAND
YON
WALKER POINT
YENT
SHIELDS MOUND
MCKEITHEN
GREEN MOUND
CEDAR KEY
TICK ISLAND
GUANA RIVER
THURSBY
ENTERPRISE
WEEDEN ISLAND
TIERRA VERDE
BIG MOUND CITY
ENGLEWOOD
FORT CENTER
SANIBEL ISLAND
TONY'S MOUND
KEY MARCO
TURNER RIVER
KEY LARGO

Figure 9. Representative mounds and middens of the Atlantic Coast Region. Many of these features are historically or archeologically important, but either have been destroyed or are not presently managed for public visitation. (See Figure 34 for publicly accessible sites.)

Figure 10. An exposed section through Whaleback Midden, near Damariscotta, Maine, showing the density and compactness of shells typical of many large middens. (The Pictorial Studio photograph.)

represents several different species, reflecting the greater species diversity in the subtropical waters. Bivalves important in southern middens include oyster, southern quahog (*Mercenaria campechiensis*), stout tagelus (*Tagelus plebeius*), Atlantic ribbed mussel (*Geukensia demissa*) and, in Florida, the coquina (*Donax variabilis*). Gastropods — especially whelks and conchs (*Busycon* spp., *Melongena corona, Pleuroploca gigantea,* and *Strombus gigas*) — are also common components of shell middens.

Shell middens were primarily refuse dumps, but some were put to other uses as well. Horticulture was sometimes practiced on level sheet middens, called **shell fields** by Jeffries Wyman, to take advantage of the accumulated lime. Shells were often placed around the base of dwelling structures, probably to hold the base of the material covering the frame in place or to provide added protection against wind, rain, or snow. When the dwelling was taken down or otherwise destroyed, the shells often remained as **hut rings.** In some coastal areas, especially in the southeastern states, mounded or ridged middens provided elevated surfaces drier than the surrounding area and were used as dwelling surfaces or sites for public structures. Sometimes human burials were made in middens.

Shell mounds, in the narrow sense of the term, are structures built of shell intended for ceremonial or other functional uses. Some shell mounds were deliberately shaped middens (including the usual non-shell debris), whereas others consisted only of clean shell. The very fact that some middens were piled high — up to 30'-35' in some cases in Florida — implies that some purpose for the design was in mind, but such purpose is not known. Some platform mounds in Florida (e.g., at Key Marco) were built with the lower part being shell midden and the higher part being formed entirely of clean shell. Burials were occasionally made by placing a low mound of clean shell over the remains of the person being interred. (Normally, the use of the term "shell mound" is broader and more inclusive than its use in this paragraph.)

Shell rings are large circular middens, varying from about 100' to 300' in diameter and up to 10' in height (Figure 11). The thickness and height of the walls of the individual rings are remarkably uniform. The surfaces enclosed by the rings are conspicuously free of midden and other habitation material. Shell rings occur along the Atlantic Coast from Charleston County, South Carolina, to Guana Peninsula, St. Johns County, Florida. These features date from the Late Archaic Period, between about 4,000-3,500 years ago. Antonio Waring has referred to these rings as the earliest monumental architectural features in the eastern United States. These rings have been interpreted as forts, fish traps and, more recently, habitation surfaces and middens associated with circular village plans.

Several islands (keys) located off the southwest coast of Florida between Charlotte Harbor and Key Marco contain extensive land reclamation and surface contouring complexes that are called **key dweller** sites (Figure 12). These sites are frequently referred to as **pile dweller** sites, or **shellworks,** even though neither term is accurate for the entire set of features found at any one site. The surface area of many of these keys has been increased artificially — and sometimes extensively — through the accu-

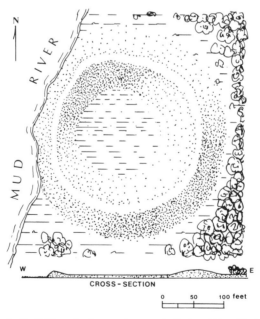

Figure 11. The Sapelo Shell Ring, the largest known shell ring. (After Waring and Larson, 1977.)

26

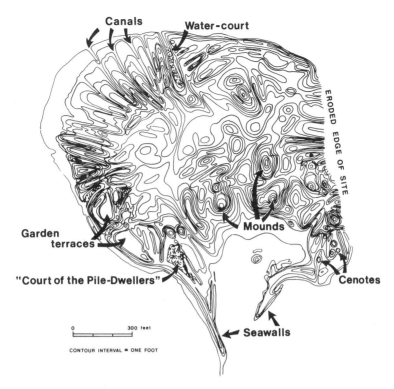

Figure 12. Key Marco, the most widely known key dweller site on the southwest Florida coast. Some representative key dweller landscape structures are identified on this contour map, redrawn from Cushing's report on the site. This site has been almost completely destroyed by urban development. (After Cushing, 1897 and Gilliland, 1975.)

mulation of midden debris (and perhaps through deliberate landfilling) that resulted in an outward expansion of the islands. Shell middens proper, burial mounds, platform mounds, and perhaps domiciliary, or house, mounds constitute the raised features found at these sites. Breakwaters were built to protect bays. Other typical surface modifications include canals which led toward the island center and often terminated in court-like landings. Sunken roads, graded ways, and walks connected some features on the islands. Cenotes (circular wells) were dug for obtaining fresh-water. Courtyards were located near the platform mounds. Parts of the islands were terraced. Some features on these islands were made entirely from the shells of millions of conch (*Busycon* spp.) piled together to make true shell mounds. Other features were embellished with a facade of conch shells; the pointed end of the shells was stuck into the feature, leaving a facing formed entirely of the broad, spiral end of contiguous shells. The age of these shellworks is not well known, but indications are that some of the islands were occupied from about 500 B.C. until the 18th Century. Some form of artificial contouring was probably carried out during all periods of occupancy.

27

Stone Mounds, or **cairns,** are conical, elliptical, or columnar piles of cobbles. In the Atlantic Coast Region, these features occur irregularly from New York to Florida, and may represent several different functions (trail markers, local monuments, rocks cleared from planted fields, etc.). Most stone mounds, however, were probably burial mounds — low stone coverings placed over the graves of one or more persons. Some burial cairns enclose single or multiple vaults. Stone mounds occur singly or in clusters, and range from small nearly imperceptible piles to mounds 100′ long or 10′ high. Most aboriginal stone mounds are considered to be of Woodland origin (Figure 13). (Some stone mounds in the Atlantic Coast Region are known to be or suspected of being of Euro-American origin.)

Figure 13. The T. F. Nelson Mound, Caldwell County, North Carolina, as excavated by John P. Rogan and aides as part of the Bureau of Ethnology's Mound Explorations. At least three different types of stone cysts were used to encapsulate burials in this unusual sunken graveyard. (From Thomas, 1894.)

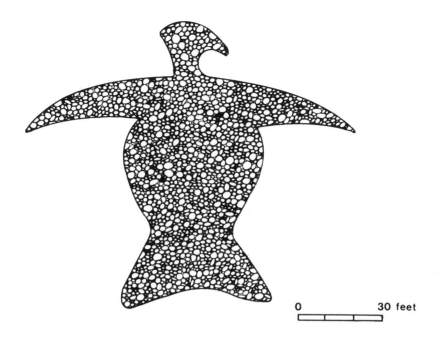

0   30 feet

Figure 14. Rock Eagle, a stone effigy mound of probable Middle Woodland age, located in Putnam County, Georgia.

Stone effigy mounds are a special category of stone mound. These are typically rendered in the form of an animal — usually a bird or a serpent. The best known stone effigy mounds in the Atlantic Coast Region are in Putnam County, Georgia (Figure 14). These mounds might have been burial monuments with additional ceremonial significance attached, but their true meaning is not known. Most stone effigies are considered to be of Woodland origin.

Stone walls or **stone enclosures** are linear or polygonal features built of cobbles (Figure 15). In the Atlantic states, these walls are restricted to the Appalachian Highlands, where they are often — but not exclusively — located near or around the top of hills or peaks. Their courses and shapes have been influenced by the local topography. The upland location and placement of these walls suggests that they were intended to control access to the hilltops or peaks. Consequently, these are often called "forts;" they could have been used for defense, for regulated (or unregulated) ceremonial functions, or for other purposes.

Prehistoric **earthen mounds** are raised architectural features that occur throughout most of the eastern United States. These mounds are most frequently made of soil and other fine sediments (clay, sand, and fine gravel), but they occasionally include cobbles or shells. Conical and plat-

Figure 15. Fort Mountain Stone Wall, Murray County, Georgia, is representative of stone walls and enclosures that occurred throughout much of the southern Appalachian Highlands.

form mounds occur in the Atlantic Coast Region; farther west, earthen effigy mounds also occur.

Most earthen mounds are circular to elliptical at the base and are rounded to subrounded across the summit (Figure 16). These conical and elliptical mounds were built most frequently as burial monuments, but they also were used as foundations for houses (or other structures) and for ceremonial purposes (e.g., platforms for charnel houses, crematoria, and possibly observatories). These mounds vary from scarcely perceptible rises to — in Ohio and West Virginia — massive earthen cones nearly 70′ high. The construction of artificial earthen burial mounds in the eastern United States began during the Early Woodland Period and reached its greatest geographic extent during the Middle Woodland Period, although the practice continued in some areas into the Historic Period. Burial mound construction was practiced throughout the Atlantic Coast Region but was rare in New England (and the Maritime Provinces), and was relatively uncommon from New York to Maryland.

Mound burials and mound construction varied considerably in detail. Some burial mounds were built as a single event, but more commonly they were built in discrete stages as the need arose for additional interments (Figure 17). Some burial mounds contained only one grave; most contained multiple graves, and some held the remains of hundreds of bodies (Figure 18). Burials were made in the floor of the original ground surface, on the original ground surface, on an existing mound surface, in the existing mound, and in newly added mound material. Some persons were buried in

Figure 16. Romney Mound, located in Indian Mound Cemetery, Romney, West Virginia, is representative of the thousands of small Middle and Late Woodland burial mounds that occurred throughout much of eastern North America.

the flesh — in either extended or flexed positions — while others were defleshed before being interred (Figure 19). The skeletons of defleshed corpses were sometimes interred in anatomically correct order and position (Figure 20) and, at other times, as bundles of bones. Bodies or skeletons were usually interred singly, but sometimes mass burial was practiced. Occasionally, decapitated skeletons or skulls only were buried. Some remains were cremated. Uncremated or cremated remains were sometimes placed in log tombs, stone tombs, or ceramic burial urns, or beneath a core mound of gravel or shells. The material of mound construction reflected the availability of local sediments, so sand mounds are especially common on the Coastal Plain, while mixtures of soils and other sediments were used to build mounds in alluvial valleys and upland areas.

Conical house mounds and ceremonial platform mounds were most common in the southeastern states. The house mounds provided elevated living surfaces in areas where high water tables or periodic floods made natural dwelling surfaces less desirable. Conical ceremonial platform mounds might indicate either local innovation, or early diffusion from Mesoamerica, of the idea of elevating religious structures on mounds.

Platform mounds usually vary from square to elongated rectangles at the base and have the form of truncated pyramids (Figures 21, 22). Monks Mound at Cahokia, Illinois, the largest platform mound in the United States, measures about 1,000′ by 800′ at the base. The largest platform mound in the Atlantic Coastal Region is Mound A at Etowah, Georgia, which meas-

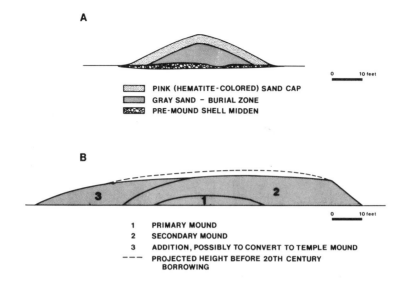

A

☐ PINK (HEMATITE-COLORED) SAND CAP
▨ GRAY SAND – BURIAL ZONE
▨ PRE-MOUND SHELL MIDDEN

0   10 feet

B

3   1   2

1   PRIMARY MOUND
2   SECONDARY MOUND
3   ADDITION, POSSIBLY TO CONVERT TO TEMPLE MOUND
– – –   PROJECTED HEIGHT BEFORE 20TH CENTURY
         BORROWING

0   10 feet

Figure 17. Representative cross-sections of Woodland burial mounds from the Atlantic Coast Region. A — Walker Point Mound, Amelia Island, Florida. This mound was built as one event. B — Barnhill Mound, Palm Beach County, Florida. This mound was constructed in at least three phases. Both mounds were damaged prior to excavation by professional archeologists, so the actual contour of the mounds before disturbance has been estimated. (After Hemmings and Deagan, 1973 and Bullen, 1957.)

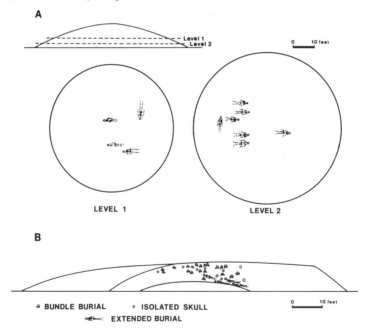

A

Level 1
Level 2

0   10 feet

LEVEL 1   LEVEL 2

B

∆ BUNDLE BURIAL   ○ ISOLATED SKULL
⊶ EXTENDED BURIAL

0   10 feet

Figure 18. Representative burial patterns in mounds of the Atlantic Coast Region. A — Hollywood Mound, Georgia. B — Barnhill Mound, Florida. (After Thomas, 1894 and Bullen, 1950.)

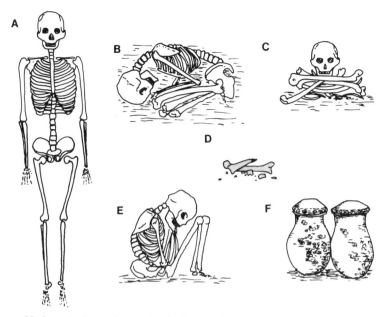

Figure 19. Some burial modes used in the Atlantic Coast Region. A — Extended primary; B — Flexed primary; C — Bundle; D — Cremated; E — Seated primary; F — Urn (skeletal remains and/or ashes inside urns). See also Figure 18.

Figure 20. A log tomb burial found in the funeral mound at Ocmulgee National Monument. This skeleton was defleshed, then rearticulated for burial. (National Park Service, Ocmulgee National Monument photograph.)

Figure 21. The Great and Lesser Temple Mounds, Early Mississippi platform mounds on the edge of the Macon Plateau at Ocmulgee National Monument, Bibb County, Georgia. Railroad construction in the 1840s destroyed part of the Lesser Temple Mound (see Figure 22). The pentagonal feature marks the site of an English trading post established in 1690. (National Park Service, Ocmulgee National Monument photograph.)

ures about 350' by 275' at the base. Platform mounds vary in height from a few feet to 66' at Etowah Mound A and 100' at Monks Mound. Low platform mounds could have been built as one event, but larger mounds were enlarged one or more times (Figure 23). The reasons for periodic enlargement of these mounds are not clear, but appear to be related to replacement of the ceremonial structures located on the mound or to replacement of the leaders who occupied the platform structure(s). When enlarged, the old mound surface would be restored and perhaps elevated,new earthen material would be added to enlarge the base and sides, and then often the surface would be sealed with clay. Sometimes burials of deceased leaders and their retainers or relatives would be made in the platform mounds. Some multiple stage mounds indicate that the structures that occupied previous platform surfaces were burned before enlargement took place. Evidence from some sites in Georgia and Florida, such as Kolomoki and Crystal River, indicate that platform mounds probably were being built by Late Woodland Tradition Weeden Island people. However, platform mounds are most closely associated with the Mississippian Tradition.

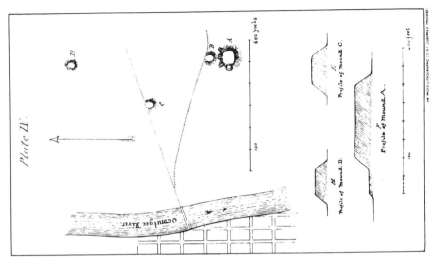

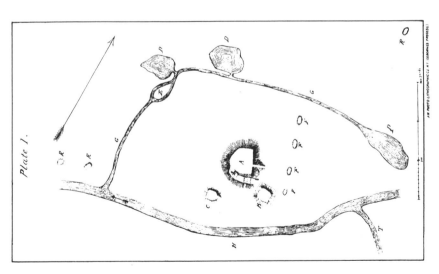

Figure 22. The Etowah (Plate I) and Ocmulgee (Plate IV) mound groups as presented in Jones, 1873. In both illustrations, Mound A is the primary temple mound and Mound C is the major burial, or funeral, mound. Railroad construction through the Ocmulgee Site in the 1840s and 1870s damaged the smaller temple mound (B) and the funeral mound (C).

35

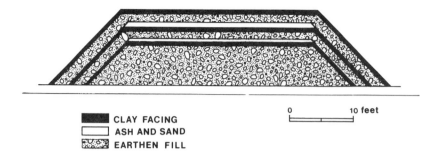

CLAY FACING
ASH AND SAND
EARTHEN FILL

0   10 feet

Figure 23. A schematic cross section through a Mississippian platform mound showing the process of mound enlargement through the addition of successive layers.

Platform mounds also occur as truncated cones and other geometric forms. The cone pattern is well represented in the Appalachian Summit Region (Figure 24), but other forms occur sporadically.

Earthworks are raised earthen features that occur in many different forms, including single walls, parallel walls, circles, squares, octagons, other regular polygons and irregular closed embankments. Some earthworks enclosed or partly bordered functional areas, such as game yards, public plazas, ceremonial space, burial grounds, or residential areas. Most earthworks, however, are not so clearly associated with a function and their actual purposes are not known. Some, similar to some stone walls, surround hilltops or peaks and suggest an isolating function; these have been called "forts" and are frequently referred to as hilltop enclosures. In eastern North America, earthworks were constructed by Indians of the Late Archaic, Woodland, and Mississippian Periods.

Various types of earthworks occur in the Atlantic Coast Region. Perhaps the most elaborate are the **big circle** sites of the Belle Glade Phase in the Lake Okeechobee Basin of south Florida. Here, between 500 B.C. and A.D. 500, in one of the earliest Woodland cultural climaxes of eastern North America, were built large and diverse mound and earthwork complexes. Conical ceremonial platform mounds, conical domiciliary mounds, and perhaps rectangular platform domiciliary mounds were built at these sites. Earthworks were formed of soil, sand, and rock alongside ditches that had been cut through the underlying impervious hardpan presumably to allow soil to drain. The ditches, and their bordering earthworks, were formed in circular, linear, and radial patterns; the drained fields were used as living and ceremonial areas or were planted in crops, including maize. Linear, circular, and sinuous earthen walls, and enclosures, are also known from the Belle Glade sites. After approximately A.D. 500, long linear embankments were constructed as **raised fields** which were well-drained and possibly used for habitation surfaces, ceremonial functions, or agricultural fields (Figure 25).

Other Woodland earthworks in the Atlantic Coast Region include "geometric" earthworks in Florida, Georgia and South Carolina (Figure 26). The functions of these features is unknown, but is presumed to have been ceremonial. Some sunken roads in Florida were paralleled by bordering earthen walls. Many Mississippian settlement sites included parallel walls bordering game ("chunkey") fields and enclosures surrounding larger ceremonial areas (Figure 24). In the northeastern states, palisaded villages of Woodland Indians often included low earthen walls as foundations for the palisade posts. These foundations remain as earthen traces of the former location of village stockades.

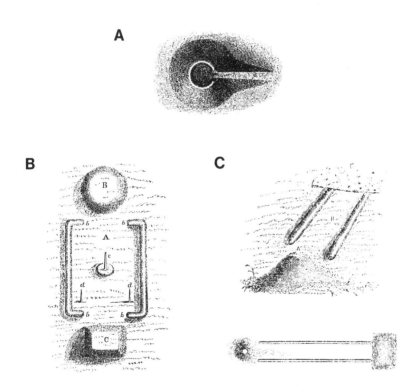

Figure 24. Mississippian mounds and earthworks from the southern Atlantic Coast Region. A — A conical platform mound representative of many — such as Nikwasi — found in western North Carolina and environs. B — A generalized rendition of the Mississippian ceremonial "chunk yard." C — Two perspectives on the Mount Royal site, Florida, including the mound, the sunken ceremonial way with paralleling walls, and the artificial pond. All views are from Squier and Davis, 1848; B and C (and possibly A) are based on sketches by William Bartram.

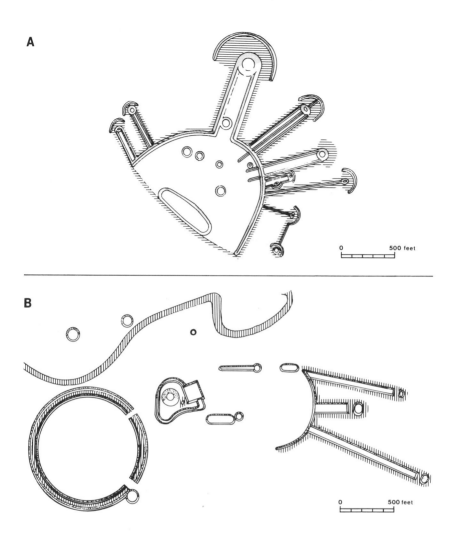

Figure 25. Two examples of *big circle* earthworks representative of the Belle Glade Phase, Lake Okeechobee Basin, Florida. A — Big Mound City. B — Fort Center. (After Morgan, 1980.)

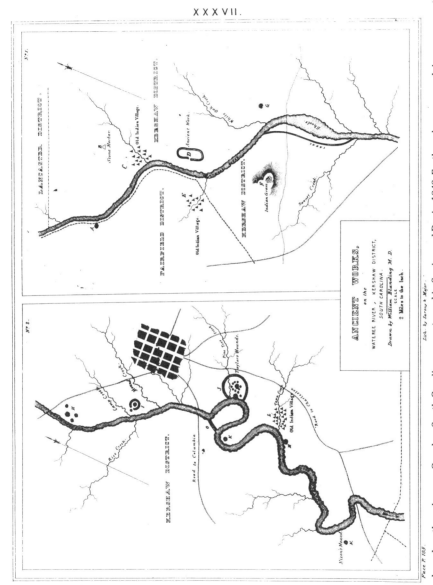

Figure 26. Mounds and earthworks near Camden, South Carolina, as portrayed in Squier and Davis, 1848. Earthworks were much less common than mounds in the Atlantic Coast region, and were typically much less complex than those found in the Mississippi Valley.

MOUNDS AND MIDDENS DURING THE HISTORIC PERIOD

European adventurers exploring the Atlantic and Gulf coasts of what are now the United States and Canada, and the settlers that followed, were quick to notice the numerous shell middens and mounds that occurred in this region. Alvar Nuñez Cabeza de Vaca wrote of seeing, along the west coast of Florida in 1528, houses of Indians made ". . .of mats set up on masses of oyster shells, which they sleep upon." Twenty one years later, within days after landing at Tampa Bay, the expedition of Hernando de Soto entered the Indian town of Ucita — a town of "seven or eight houses, built of timber, and covered with palm leaves. The chief's house stood near the beach, upon a very high mound made by hand for defense. . ." The first paintings of mounds from the Atlantic Coast Region (Figure 27) were made by Jacques Le Moyne, a member of the short-lived French Huguenot colony that attempted to settle in 1564 at Fort Caroline, along the lower St. Johns River, Florida. As exploration and settlement by Dutch, English, French, and other European interests got underway to the north of Florida, similar observations appeared. "Lime they make of oyster shells, great heaps of which are found here, made formerly by the savages, who subsist in part by that fishery," wrote Fr. Isaac Jogues in reference to the Dutch colonists of Long Island during the middle part of the 17th Century.

One and one-half centuries of observations along the Atlantic and Gulf coasts indicate that the Europeans recognized that (1) mounds and middens were built by humans and (2) they were perceived to fulfill certain functions (dwelling surfaces, burial monuments, defense) or were by-products of specific activities (shellfishing). European encroachment led to the rapid demise of native cultures, however, and mound- and midden-building came to an end relatively soon after contact was established in any given region. Consequently, the popular awareness of the origins and functions of mounds and middens was lost, and uncertainty and mystery about these features developed. During the 17th Century, pragmatic attitudes toward the mounds and middens dominated among the colonists. These features were seen increasingly as readily available sources of raw materials or as physical obstructions that needed to be removed.

Figure 27. This painting of an Indian leader's grave by Jacques LeMoyne is the earliest known graphic rendition of a North American Indian mound. It is based on observations made by LeMoyne while at the the ill-fated French Huguenot colony of La Caroline, located near the mouth of the St. Johns River, Florida, in 1564-1565. (From Bennett, 1968.)

REAWAKENED CURIOSITY

Renewed interest in the mounds appeared in the English colonies after the middle of the 18th Century. English penetration of the Ohio Valley especially increased following the end of the French and Indian War in 1763, when England gained control of almost all land east of the Mississippi River. English exploration of the Ohio Valley led to the discovery of many large and complex mounds and earthworks. These features were the products of Adena and Ohio Hopewell Indians, and were far more numerous and spectacular than the smaller, simpler mounds known from the middle Atlantic colonies. England also acquired Florida from Spain in 1763. That fact, along with the spread of English influence and control over the southeastern Indians inland from the southern colonies, made the Carolinas, Georgia, and Florida safer and more attractive destinations for travelers from the English colonies.

Accounts of the Ohio Valley mounds began to appear during the 1770s. These reports usually did not bear directly on mounds of the Atlantic Coast Region, but they did stimulate considerable interest in mounds. The most important source of information about mounds of the Atlantic Coast Region prepared during this period was William Bartram's book, *Travels through North and South Carolina, Georgia, East and West Florida...*, published in 1791. Bartram spent nearly five years (1773-1778) traveling through the southeast observing the natural history of the region. Woven into the fabric of his *Travels. . .* are references to mound sites that vary from incidental comments to descriptions presented with artistic detail. The last three pages of this classic publication in American natural history summarize the "Languages and Manners" of the southeastern Indians; most of this summary is concerned with mounds and mound-like features of the region through which Bartram traveled.

An important pioneering investigation in the scientific study of mounds, and an historically significant step in the development of American archeology, was undertaken in 1784 by Thomas Jefferson. Jefferson's account of this work was included in the only book-length publication he authored — *Notes on the State of Virginia,* published in 1787. Jefferson knew of several small mounds near his home at Monticello in Albemarle County, and elsewhere, in Virginia. These were accepted as burial mounds by the Americans but the manner in which burials were made, and the reason(s) for the burials, were unconfirmed and speculation on these questions had given rise to a body of folklore.

"That they were repositories of the dead, has been obvious to all: but on what particular occasion constructed, was matter of doubt. Some have thought they covered the bones of those who have fallen in battles fought on the spot of interment. Some ascribed them to the custom, said to prevail among the Indians, of collecting, at certain periods, the bones of all their dead, wheresoever deposited at the time of death. Others again suppose them the general sepulchres for towns, conjectured to have been on or near these grounds; and this opinion was supported by the quality of the lands in which they are found, (those constructed of earth being generally in the softest and most fertile meadow-grounds on river sides) and by a tradition, said to be handed down from the Aboriginal Indians, that, when they settled in a town, the first person who died was placed erect, and earth put about him, so as to cover and support him; that, when another died, a narrow passage was dug to the first, the second reclined against him, and the cover of earth replaced, and so on. There being one of these in my neighbourhood, I wished to satisfy myself whether any, and which of these opinions were just. For this purpose I determined to open and examine it thoroughly." (Jefferson, 1787, pp. 97-98)

Jefferson sampled the mound by sinking several shallow pits into it at various places, and then by cutting a trench completely through the mound, near the center, to the original ground level. Among his observations were that the bones of humans were deposited (1) from the original ground surface to the uppermost parts of the mound (2) in stratified layers, (3) that bones in the upper levels were less decayed than those in lower levels, and (4) that bones of children and adults were present. He concluded that the mound had been enlarged periodically, and that bones appeared to have been collected from other locations and subsequently placed in the mound. Jefferson found no evidence of upright burials or injuries as might be sustained by warriors killed in battle. The scientific importance of Jefferson's investigation of this mound is that he formulated a question or problem to be investigated (how are Indians buried in mounds), made systematic observations and collected data from those observations, analyzed the data collected, and reached conclusions based on the analysis.

Learned societies began to appear in the eastern United States during the late part of the 18th and first half of the 19th Century, and some of these played important roles in the developing study of mounds. One of the earliest and most important of these societies was the American Philosophical Society, established in 1769 in Philadelphia. Thomas Jefferson was president of this Society from 1797 to 1814. In 1799, Jefferson instituted a survey of archeological remains of the United States, requesting his correspondents, among other things, "to obtain accurate plans, drawings and descriptions of...ancient Fortifications, Tumuli, and other Indian work of art." The American Antiquarian Society was established in Boston, Massachusetts, in 1812, with expressed interest in the Ohio mounds. When this Society started publication of its *Transactions and Collections* in 1820, much of the first issue was devoted to Caleb Atwater's pioneering regional synthesis "Description of the antiquities discovered in the State of Ohio and other western states." Later, in 1842, the American Ethnological Society was established through the influence of Albert Gallatin. In 1845, this Society commissioned Ephraim George Squier, editor of *The Chillicothe Gazette* in Chillicothe, Ohio, to compile information for a definitive study of the mounds. This study was completed, with the assistance of Dr. Edwin H. Davis of Chillicothe, in 1847 but was so extensive and lavishly illustrated that the American Ethnological Society could not afford to publish it. The manuscript — *Ancient Monuments of the Mississippi Valley* — was accepted for publication by the youthful Smithsonian Institution (created in 1845) as the first title in its *Contributions to Knowledge.* Squier and Davis's study dealt mainly with the mounds and earthworks of the Ohio Valley, but it did include some information about mounds in other areas — including North Carolina, South Carolina and Florida among the Atlantic states (Figures 24, 26). In addition to publishing *Ancient Monuments of the Mississippi Valley* in 1848, the Smithsonian Institution quickly became the most important scholarly institution involved with the study of mounds during the remainder of the 19th Century, and was an important catalyst of progress in the scientific study of these archeological resources.

SCIENTIFIC STUDY OF MOUNDS AND MIDDENS

When the mining of shell middens for agricultural lime increased during the first half of the 19th Century, scholarly interest in these features was aroused. One of the first questions addressed was whether these piles of shell were natural or artificial structures. Such vast quantities of shell, sometimes in what appeared to be stratified layers, suggested to some observers that these were natural accumulations deposited in flowing water or coastal depressions and subsequently uplifted. Others — such as Lardner Vanuxem and Paul Chadbourne — responded that the heaps in question were almost exclusively products of human activity, noting that the middens contained charcoal and ashes; other cultural debris such as pottery, stone tools, remains of food animals; and that they rested upon the same soil as the surrounding terrain.

Scientific study of shell middens in Denmark during the 1850s provided examples of work that could be emulated by scholars in the United States. In 1861, the Smithsonian Institution published a translation of a summary of this European work by A. Morlot. This publication stimulated much study of middens in the United States and Canada, particularly — in the Atlantic region — in the Maritime Provinces and the states of Maine, Massachusetts, and Florida. Eminent among the Americans who studied shell middens during the 1860s and 1870s was Jeffries Wyman, first curator (1866-1874) of the Peabody Museum of American Archaeology and Ethnology at Harvard University. Wyman studied middens in New England and Florida, and his publication *Fresh-Water Shell Mounds of the St. John's River, Florida* is a classic study of shell midden archeology. In this work, Wyman provided extensive descriptions of many middens along the St. Johns River, concluded that these features were enlarged over extended periods of time, and established a simple but valid and enduring chronology for the prehistory of the region based on ceramic evidence (or the lack of it) from the middens (Figure 28). To the north, George Matthew's review of excavations conducted at Bocabec, New Brunswick, was published in 1884 as "Discoveries at a village of the stone age at Bocabec, N.B." This pioneering article presented conclusions about the detailed use by Indians of the Bocabec middens, including dwelling sites, village plan, and seasonal activities. This article has been called the finest piece of archeological field work carried out in eastern Canada in the 19th Century.

While shell middens were being described, discussed, and analyzed, mounds and earthworks were the focus of a persistent speculative, and sometimes raging, controversy about their origins. Many people — scholars and others — believed that the mounds were built not by American Indians but by some lost civilization of Mound Builders. The romantic and nationalistic appeal of this argument was well received by many people. Canaanites, Vikings, Hindus, Romans, Phoenicians, and others were put forth as possible candidates for the Lost Race of Mound Builders. The Indians with which the American settlers from the middle and northern Atlantic Coast came into contact were themselves usually unaware of who had built the mounds. In addition, the Americans perceived the historic Indians as lacking the organizational and technological skills necessary to build the large and complex mounds encountered in the Mississippi (including Ohio) Valley. Throughout the debate, sober opposition to the notion of a Lost Race of Mound Builders had been present, if not heard or heeded. Thomas Jefferson was an early advocate of the idea that the mounds were built by Indians. Dr. J. H. McCulloch, Jr., of Baltimore and Samuel G. Morton of Philadelphia presented this same view during the first half of the 19th Century, as did Samuel F. Haven and Henry R. Schoolcraft after mid-Century.

In 1879, the Bureau of Ethnology was created within the Smithsonian Institution, and John Wesley Powell was appointed its Director. Two years later, Congress stipulated that $5,000 of the Bureau's current budget should be spent on the study of mounds. Powell was opposed to the study of North American archeology within the Bureau, but nonetheless followed the mandate and created the Division of Mound Exploration. Wills de Haas was placed in charge of this Division, but he resigned shortly thereafter and was replaced by Cyrus Thomas, who directed the unit throughout its 13-year history (1881-1894). Thomas was instructed to determine, above all else, whether the mounds had been built by American Indians or by some other group. Thomas approached this problem by sending teams into different parts of the eastern United States to collect information about mounds representative of different geographic regions. Reports of progress during the course of the investigations were published by the Bureau, but the most important single publication to come from the survey was Cyrus Thomas' summary of the Division's work — *Report on the Mound Explorations of the Bureau of Ethnology.* The *Report. . .,* published in 1894, described (1) the different kinds of mounds and mound-like features recognized by Thomas and (2) the sites investigated during the study, (3) identified different mound regions, and (4) concluded with a lengthy, detailed analysis of the evidence collected bearing on the identity of the people who built the mounds. Thomas' conclusion was that the mounds had been built by Indians, and by several different groups of Indians at that. Thomas' *Report. . .,* more than any other single document, signaled the end of the myth of the Lost Race of Mound Builders. Simultaneously, it became one of the cornerstones of professional archeology.

Clarence B. Moore was a wealthy businessman from Philadelphia. Upon retiring, Moore financed and directed his own investigations of southeastern mounds and middens and, in doing so, wrote his own chapter in the history of southeastern archeology. Each winter, from 1892 to 1913, Moore traveled by houseboat along the Atlantic or Gulf coast, or on various rivers, examining the mounds and middens of the region. Reports were prepared following each seasons's fieldwork and most were quickly published, at Moore's expense, in the *Journal of the Academy of Natural Sciences of Philadelphia*. Moore's investigations were not carried out with the best of techniques, but they did contribute much new information about mounds and middens in a region that had been — and for some time would continue to be — relatively neglected in the study of American antiquities. (Forty five maps of Moore's survey routes and sites are in B. W. Bierer's *Indians and Artifacts in the Southeast,* pp. 293-336.)

The archeological study of the mounds and middens during the 20th Century has shifted away from describing features and their artifacts. Progressively, more emphasis has been placed upon establishing cultural characteristics, differences, and change among mound building groups; the chronology and age of the cultural groups recognized; demographic, economic, and ecologic patterns of the groups; and inter-regional dynamics — such as the content and operations of regional trade networks and the diffusion of cultural elements. These questions have been investigated by many archeologists, reflecting the rapid growth and professionalization of archeology during the 20th Century; representative contributions from these archeologists are identified in Section III — Publications.

PERCEPTION AND ALTERATION OF MOUNDS AND MIDDENS DURING THE HISTORIC PERIOD

At the onset of European colonization of the Atlantic seaboard, there was a larger number of mounds and similar structures in the United States and Canada than ever before or since. Today, there are fewer of these features than at any time during the last 2,500-3,000 years. Some of the mounds and middens have been destroyed or altered by natural processes, especially erosion (Figure 28). Coastal sites have been, and are being, destroyed by rising sea level. Among accessible sites, Kidder Point (Maine) and Spanish Mount (South Carolina) show the effect of coastal erosion especially well. Stream erosion, by lateral shifts of the stream channel and floods, has damaged many inland mounds. The large Rembert Mound along the Savannah River in Elbert County, Georgia — once more than 30' high and several hundred yards in circumference — was largely destroyed by a single flood in 1908. The mounds at Chattahoochee Landing (Florida) are examples of surviving mounds that have been damaged by floods. Tree fall, burrowing by rodents, and even earthquakes are among other natural processes that alter mounds and middens.

The most extensive and rapid cause of mound and midden destruction, however, has been the human alteration of these features. Shell fields were cultivated by Europeans just as they had been by Indians. The Nauset Marsh Site (Massachusetts) is one such area that was plowed and planted

Figure 28. A large shell midden at Old Enterprise along the north shore of Lake Monroe on the St. Johns River, Florida, as it appeared in 1874. Part of this midden had been destroyed by wave action; the remaining part was removed for fertilizer and walkway and road construction. (From Wyman, 1875.)

so frequently during the historic period that surface evidence of midden deposits, while never extensive, has been obliterated entirely. Probably the most widespread and common use of midden shell, prior to the late part of the 19th Century, was for the manufacture of lime. "At the mouth of Pickawaxent Creek, about eighty miles below Washington, there is an extensive deposit of oyster shells at which an establishment has been formed, which, in a few months has converted many thousand bushels of them into lime" wrote Lardner Vanuxem in 1843. Agricultural use of lime increased substantially following agricultural reform during the first quarter of the 19th Century. Lime was also used extensively in masonry construction; many surviving old masonry buildings from Maine to Florida are held together with mortar made with midden lime (Figure 29). Tabby, a cement containing lime, sand or gravel, and shell, was used extensively for construction along the coast of South Carolina, Georgia, and northern Florida during the 17th and 18th centuries. Dried shell from middens was preferred for tabby because the lime was more easily released and less salt was present than in fresh shell. Ruins of tabby buildings can be seen on Sapelo Island (as part of the tour that includes the shell ring) as well as at numerous other historic sites and historic districts along the coast of the south Atlantic states (Figure 30).

From early colonial time into the 20th Century, shell was often used to surface walks and roads. After macadamized surfaces came into use in the 19th Century, midden shell was used as both subsurface gravel and filler in the surfacing material. This use increased significantly during the 20th

Figure 29. Lime from midden shells was used to make mortar for the construction of Castillo de San Marcos, initially built by the Spanish (partly upon a shell midden) at St. Augustine, Florida, after 1671. (Susan L. Woodward photograph.)

Figure 30. Ruins of the Major William Horton House on Jekyll Island, Georgia. This house was built of *tabby* during the 1740s. Numerous shells are visible where the plaster finish has separated near this second floor window. (Jekyll Island Authority photograph.)

Century with the popularization of the automobile and the subsequent need to better maintain both paved and unpaved roads. Heavy use of midden shell for road building continued until after World War II, but has been decreasing significantly since. Sewee Shell Ring (South Carolina) and Castle Windy Midden (Florida) are examples of shell features that were partly mined for road building purposes.

Some middens have been altered or destroyed in more unusual ways. Most of the Whaleback Midden (Maine) was shipped to Boston in 1886 to be pulverized and sold as chicken feed (Figure 31). Several middens around Chesapeake Bay, and probably others near oyster-producing areas elsewhere, were used as cultch — material put down in the oyster beds to which the young oysters attach. One large midden near Fort Walton Beach, Florida, was allegedly used as a fort by the southern army during the Civil War, and the Arrowhead Middens on Mullet Key, Florida, were part of a bombing and gunnery range during World War II.

Like middens, mounds were often mined for sand and shell, primarily for use in road and building construction. Other mounds were damaged or destroyed by cultivation — they usually having been perceived as impediments to farming that should be leveled as quickly as possible. Some platform mounds were too high and steep-sided to be cultivated, so they were spared leveling by the plow. Some farmers, however, did cultivate the platform surfaces of some mounds, such as those at Etowah. Other structures, such as the Enterprise Mound (midden, Florida) (Figure 28), or the platform mound at Chattahoochee Landing, had buildings built on top of them. Reservoir construction, the building of transportation systems and urbanization have taken a heavy toll of mounds and have caused the loss of or damage to many middens (Figure 22). Mounds and middens have also been

Figure 31. Whaleback Midden, along the Damariscotta River, Maine, being mined in 1886. Shell from this midden was ground and sold as chicken feed in Boston. (The Pictorial Studio photograph.)

lost to military activities and recreational abuse (especially walking on steep sides and vehicular traffic). Artifact collectors, amateur archeologists, and even professional archeologists have contributed to the reduction of both middens and mounds, especially prior to the development of modern investigative strategies and ethics, management objectives, and public awareness.

PROTECTION AND MANAGEMENT OF ARCHEOLOGICAL RESOURCES IN THE PUBLIC INTEREST

Increasingly, archeological resources — sites and the material artifacts and other information they contain — are being viewed as public resources that should be protected and managed in the public interest. On one level, this is true because many people within society enjoy seeing artifacts, visiting sites, and understanding how, why, and when these records of other cultures were produced (Figure 32). On another level is the opinion that all of society stands to benefit from a clearer, more complete understanding of the past. A more complete understanding of what has gone before allows present conditons and future prospects to be more realistically appraised.

Much information about the prehistory of Anglo-America has been extracted from the land already. This information has contributed greatly to our current understanding of the past, and will certainly provide additional insight with further analyses and revision of thought. A great amount of data, however, is still in the ground in the numerous extant prehistoric archeological sites. As has been happening for the last 400 years, these sites are being destroyed regularly — by reservoir construction, mechanization and intensification of agriculture, transportation systems development, and urban sprawl, as well as by natural processes — and with the loss passes information that never can be replaced. Clearly, there is widespread opinion and urgency that strong steps be taken to protect additional sites in the public interest.

One important means of protecting archeological resources is through federal and state legislation, and local ordinances. Such laws extend the protection of the respective governments to archeological resources (sites, artifacts, and other associated information) (1) located on lands owned by the respective governments and, with increasing frequency, (2) on other lands that will be altered by (a) the direct activities of, or (b) activities receiving financial or administrative support from, the respective governments. Beyond protection, some federal legislation also provides extensive support for the identification, investigation, and preservation of archeological resources (Figure 33). Principal pieces of federal legislation that have protected, or supported inventory of, archeological resources are listed in Table 3. Most states now provide some form of legal protection for archeological resources on state-owned lands, and some states have provisions for extending protection to sites on municipal and private land as well. In the Atlantic Coast Region, for example, Virginia's Cave Protection Act protects archeological resources in *all* caves within the Commonwealth except those removed from privately owned caves *by* the landowner. Maine law provides that easements may be obtained by the state to privately owned archeological sites. In Pennsylvania, conditions may be imposed on the transfer of state owned or controlled lands so as to protect resources of known cultural significance under the new ownership. Florida has instituted an active program of acquiring new state lands in order to protect cultural and natural resources. Many state environmental protection laws have provisions supporting the preservation of historic resources. At a lower level, some municipalities have their own antiquities ordinances. One such example is St. Augustine's (Florida) Archaeological Preservation Ordinance, adopted December 6, 1986.

At present, essentially all archeological resources on federal, state, and municipal land are protected by one or more pieces of legislation, as are many sites on privately owned lands, by trespassing laws if not otherwise. The typical provision of laws protecting antiquities on public lands are that excavations of protected sites can be conducted only with permits from the regulating agency and that all artifacts and other data from such sites are public property and must be deposited in specified repositories. *Disturbing*

Figure 32. The earthlodge at Ocmulgee National Monument, Georgia, a publicly accessible and interpreted feature reconstructed over the floor of an authentic Middle Mississippi (Macon Plateau) earthlodge. Ocmulgee National Monument is one of the most important and best interpreted examples of mound sites in the Atlantic Coast Region that have been protected and managed in the public interest. (National Park Service, Ocmulgee National Monument photograph.)

protected sites and possessing artifacts from those sites without the necessary permits is a crime and, increasingly, the various judicial systems are recognizing and supporting the laws protecting antiquities.

Legal protection is only one way of protecting archeological resources and the information they contain. The effectiveness of laws is minimal if the administering and enforcing agencies are underfunded, understaffed, or uncommitted to their mandated purpose. Ultimately, effective protection must come from an informed and supportive public — the public that, reciprocally, is the ultimate beneficiary of the protection provided. Hopefully, this book will contribute in a small way to increasing public awareness of the significance of prehistoric cultural resources, the past and continuing loss of these resources, present management patterns, and future prospects. Those who visit the sites identified in this book, for example, will see most of the remaining mound and mound-like features that are accessible to the public today in the Atlantic Coast Region — a mere handful of sites representing the thousands that once existed. Visitors to these sites will also see much regional variation in the number of publicly accessible sites, the condition of these sites, and the level of interpretation provided. (Sources of additional information about the protection and management of archeological resources are provided in Section III under Publications, "Protection and Management: Current Views.")

Figure 33. Excavation underway at the Kidder Point Site, Maine. Kidder Point is a good example of a small, seemingly insignificant site that yielded abundant information through the use of modern research strategy and methods. Excavation of this site and analysis of the data collected were made possible by public funds from both federal and state sources. (Maine Historic Preservation Commission photograph.)

Table 3: Major Federal Legislation Relevant to the Protection of Archeological Resources

1906	Antiquities Act	Protects federally-owned sites and provides for proper curation of artifacts and information from federally-owned sites.
1935	Historic Sites and Buildings Act	Declares national policy of preserving sites, structures and objects of national significance.
1960	Reservoir Salvage Act	Authorizes salvage recovery of resources threatened with inundation by reservoirs.
1966	National Historic Preservation Act	Major legislation which, with amendments and supplements, expands and strengthens the identification, preservation and management of sites, structures, and places of national, state, and local significance.
1974	Archaeological and Historic Preservation Act	Strengthens the salvage recovery of archeological data from sites being altered by land use or construction activities receiving federal support.
1979	Archaeological Resources Protection Act	Modernizes the protection and management of archeological resources on federal land.

SECTION II

MOUNDS AND RELATED FEATURES ACCESSIBLE TO THE PUBLIC

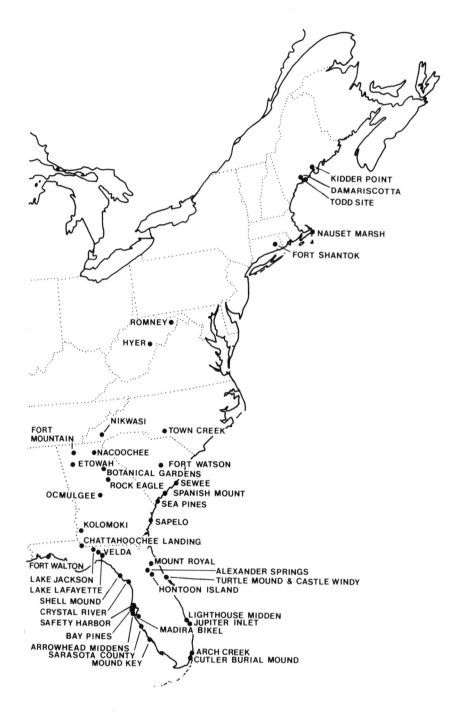

Figure 34. Publicly accessible mounds and mound-like features identified and described in Section II.

MOUNDS AND RELATED FEATURES ACCESSIBLE TO THE PUBLIC

Forty two archeological sites that include mounds, earthworks, middens, or stone works are identified and described in this Section (Figure 34, Table 4). Each site is described briefly. Detailed directions, information about public access and educational and recreational facilities (current at press time), and one or more sources of additional information are provided for each site.

The sites in this Section are arranged in geographical order, from Maine to Florida. Table 4 summarizes the major archeological features and visitor facilities found at the forty two sites.

Thirty eight of the identified sites are managed to accommodate public visitation. Many of these sites provide interpretive facilities — ranging from museums to simple information signs — and other recreational opportunities, whereas other sites function primarily to preserve rather than interpret the mounds or middens.

Four of the sites identified in this section are *not* managed to accommodate public visitation. These sites — the Damariscotta middens, Hyer Mound, Nacoochee Mound, and Lake Lafayette Mound — are included in this book because they are well known and are clearly visible from public roads. Trespassing on these sites is prohibited.

All of the sites listed in this Section are protected by law. Disturbance of these sites or removal of archeological resources is strictly prohibited.

Table 4: Features and Facilities at Sites Identified in Section II

Site	Page No.	Conical Mound	Platform Mound	Earthworks	Shell Midden	Shell Ring	Key Dweller Site	Stone Mound	Stone Wall	Stone Effigy	Reconstructed Buildings	Museum	Other Interpretation	Admission Fee[1]
Maine														
1. Kidder Point Site	60													
2. Todd Site	62				•							•		
3. Damariscotta Middens	64				•									
Massachusetts														
4. Nauset Marsh Site	67										•	•		
Connecticut														
5. Fort Shantok	69											•		P
West Virginia														
6. Romney Indian Mound	71	•												
7. Hyer Mound	72	•												
North Carolina														
8. Town Creek Mound	74		•						•		•	•		
9. Nikwasi Mound	76		•									•		
South Carolina														
10. Sewee Shell Ring	78					•								
11. Spanish Mount	80				•									
12. Sea Pines Shell Ring	82					•								•
13. Fort Watson Mound	83		•									•		

Georgia

	Site	Page									
14.	Nacoochee Mound	85	•								
15.	Fort Mountain Stone Wall	86						•		•	
16.	Etowah Mounds	88	•						•	•	
17.	Botanical Garden Mounds	91					•			•	
18.	Rock Eagle Effigy Mound	93						•		•	
19.	Ocmulgee National Monument	95		•					•	•	•
20.	Kolomoki Mounds	98	•	•					•	•	
21.	Sapelo Shell Ring	100				•					

Florida

	Site	Page									
22.	Canaveral Seashore Middens	103			•				•	•	
23.	Mount Royal	105	•						•		
24.	Alexander Springs Midden	107			•						•
25.	Hontoon Island Mound	109			•						
26.	Jupiter Inlet Lighthouse Midden	111			•			•			
27.	Jupiter Inlet Midden I	112			•				•	•	
28.	Arch Creek Midden	113			•						
29.	Cutler Burial Mound	115	•						•	•	
30.	Mound Key	117	•	•	•	•	•				•
31.	Sarasota County Mound	119			•						
32.	Madira Bickel Mounds	121	•	•					•		
33.	Arrowhead Park Middens	123			•					•	
34.	Bay Pines Mound	125	•		•					•	
35.	Safety Harbor Mound	127		•						•	
36.	Crystal River Mounds	129	•	•	•	•			•	•	M
37.	Shell Mound	132			•						
38.	Lake Lafayette Mound	133		•							
39.	Velda Mound	134		•							
40.	Lake Jackson Mounds	135		•						•	
41.	Chattahoochee Landing Mounds	137	•	•							
42.	Indian Temple Mound	139		•					•	•	M

[1] • = Admission to grounds; M = Admission to museum; P = Weekend parking.

1. Kidder Point Site

Early Woodland Shell Midden
Waldo County, Maine

The Kidder Point Site is an Early Woodland (and Historic) occupation site located on the east side of the south end of Kidder Point on land owned by Central Maine Power Company. The coast of Maine has been sinking for the last 9,000 years, and is currently doing so at the rate of about 4" each 100 years in the Kidder Point area. As a result, coastal erosion is occurring and has destroyed part of the Kidder Point Site.

Excavations were conducted at the Kidder Point Site in 1975 and 1982 (Figure 33). The site contained hearths, flakes of worked stone, remains of animals, and evidence of possible dwelling structures. Modest amounts of shellfish remains occurred at several places throughout the site, the largest accumulation being a thin sheet midden that measured up to about 15" in thickness. The shell in the sheet midden, and elsewhere in the site, was almost exclusively that of soft shell clams. Analyses of the shell and other animal remains from the middens indicate that the site probably was occupied for a single (or maybe two or three) season(s), from about March through August or September, by a small band of hunters and gatherers. The prehistoric part of this site is about 2,600-2,300 years old.

The south end of the site lies south and east of the barricade, and east of the road that bypasses the barricade enroute to the tidal flat connecting Kidder Point and Sears Island. The largest shell feature was located 0.1 mile north of the barricade, about 30 yards east of the road, just south of the red fire hydrant. The pre-excavation surface configuration of this site was restored following the excavation in 1982. The site is flat — undifferentiable from the adjacent terrain — and visitors should not expect to see raised features or exposed shell.

We have included the Kidder Point Site in this book for several reasons: (1) It is representative of the uncounted thousands of piles of ordinary shell middens that were formed by Native Americans along the Atlantic and Gulf coasts. Seeing a "featureless" site such as this allows one to better understand and appreciate the less common but better known raised features at other sites. (2) Many coastal shell middens have been, and are being, destroyed by erosion, especially as relative sea level rises. This site provides a clear illustration of just how coastal erosion can destroy a site. (3) The analysis of this site by archeologists is unusually extensive and well done, and illustrates the great amount of information about prehistoric lifestyles and material culture that can be extracted from a small, seemingly ordinary and unimportant site, using modern analytic methods and research strategies.

DIRECTIONS: From U. S. Route 1, 2 mi. E of Searsport, go 0.9 mi. S on Island Road to barricade. Site is to E of road (Figure 35).

FOR ADDITIONAL INFORMATION: Contact: Archeologist, Maine Historic Preservation Commission, 55 Capitol Street, State House Station 65, Augusta, ME 04333. **Read:** Spiess, Arthur E., and Mark H. Hedden. 1983. Kidder Point and Sears Island in Prehistory. Maine Historic Preservation Commission, Occasional Publications in Maine Archaeology, no. 3 (available from Maine Archaeological Society, P. O. Box 982, Augusta, ME 04330).

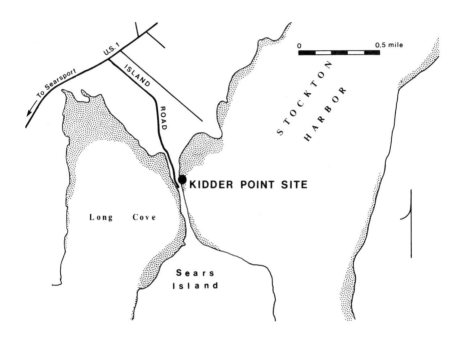

Figure 35. Location of Kidder Point Site.

2. Todd Site

Late Archaic-Woodland Shell Midden
Lincoln County, Maine

The Todd Site is located at the south end of Keene Neck, along the west shore of Muscongus Bay, on the National Audubon Society's 33 acre Todd Wildlife Sanctuary. The feature is formed primarily of the shells of soft shell clams gathered from the nearby tidal zone. This subsurface feature is about 4' thick and encompasses approximately one quarter of an acre. Exposed shell can be seen at the surface where the self-guiding Hockomock Nature Trail, one mile in length, crosses the midden.

The Todd Site midden began to accumulate about 3,800 years ago and continued in use, perhaps intermittently, until about 1,000 years ago.

DIRECTIONS: From U. S. Route 1 W of Waldoboro, go S on Maine Route 32 9 mi. to Keene Neck Road, then go SE 1.7 mi. on Keene Neck Road to Audubon Camp visitor center and Hockomock Trail on right (Figure 36).

PUBLIC USE: Season and hours: Hockomock Trail is open daily. **Fees:** None.

EDUCATIONAL FACILITIES: Visitor center: The visitor center is staffed from mid-June through August. Exhibits on bird life are on display here. **Visitor center hours:** 10:00 AM-4:00 PM daily. **Bookstore:** The visitor center offers for sale a modest selection of books and other educational materials. **Trails:** The self guiding Hockomock Nature Trail, a loop 1 mi. in length, leads from the visitor center through meadows and forest, and along the coast. The trail is marked. An interpretive trail guide, keyed to 25 identified points of interest, is available. **Staff programs:** Between mid-June and the end of August, volunteers periodically lead field trips between 10:00 AM and 4:00 PM daily.

FOR ADDITIONAL INFORMATION: Contact: Manager, Audubon Ecology Camp in Maine, Keene Neck Road, Medomak, ME 04551, 207-529-5148.

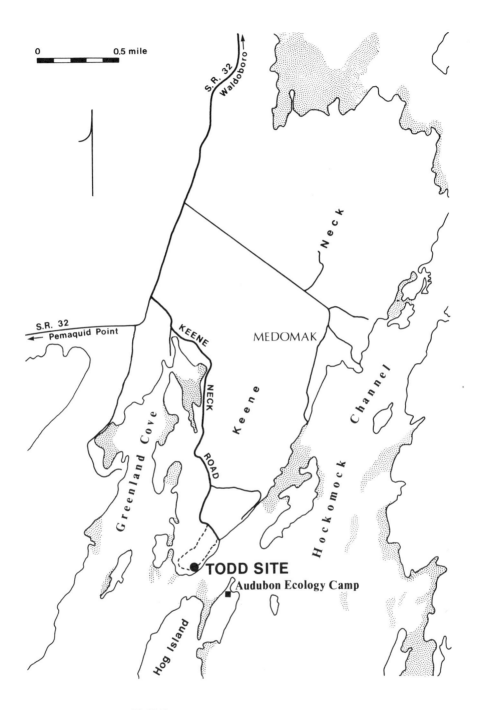

Figure 36. Location of Todd Site.

3. Damariscotta Middens

Early and Middle Woodland Shell Middens
Lincoln County, Maine

About 3,000 years ago, the rise in relative sea level brought ocean water into what is today the upper Damariscotta River and Salt Bay, creating environmental conditions there favorable for the growth of oysters. The oysters proliferated in a predator-free environment, and sometimes grew to extraordinarily large size. About 2,400 years ago, Indians began to exploit these oysters extensively. Around 1,400 years ago, however, this oyster population collapsed, possibly because of the combined effects of (1) continued rising sea level, which created a less productive environment for the oysters, and (2) the establishment of invertebrate predators in the Damariscotta oyster population. Indian use of the Damariscotta shellfish was much reduced after about 1,400 years ago.

Indians formed several shell middens over a distance of about 2 miles downstream from the mouth of Damariscotta Lake. Two of these middens were extremely large (Figure 37). Whaleback, so named because its contour reminded early American settlers of a whale, was the larger midden — described in one report as being 347' long, 123' wide, and 16' high at its maximum dimensions. Directly across the river, on the west bank, was the Peninsula, or Glidden, Midden. The Glidden Midden was about 150' long, 70' wide, and 30' deep at its maximum dimensions, although shell debris

Figure 37. Whaleback (foreground) and Glidden middens, alongside the Damariscotta River, Maine. (The Pictorial Studio photograph.)

64

was more or less continuous along this bank for about 0.5 mile. The middens were composed primarily of oyster shell; some shells were remarkably large, approaching 18″ in length.

The Damariscotta middens were considered a promising source of agricultural lime as early as the 1830s, and subsequently some of the smaller middens of the area were used for lime production. In the mid-1880s, 200 tons of shell in Whaleback were sold to a Boston company by the owner of the midden, Mrs. Stetson, at 30 cents per ton (Figures 10, 31). The shell was shipped in barrels to Boston, where it was ground and sold as poultry feed. Frederic Ward Putnam, director of the Peabody Museum at Harvard University, contracted with Abram T. Gamage in May, 1886, to salvage artifacts and other items of interest from Whaleback during the shell mining activity. Gamage worked from June until November, collecting objects and making records that constitute the most extensive and important archeological records for the Damariscotta middens. Whaleback was largely dismantled by December, 1886. Mining of the Glidden Midden was also attempted about this same time, but this was unprofitable and more recent owners have protected the site against commercial exploitation.

Presently, most of what is left of Whaleback is owned by the State of Maine, and is administered by the Bureau of Parks and Recreation. The southern part of this site is privately owned, as is all of the Glidden Midden. Neither of these sites is publicly accessible, but they can be seen from U. S. Route 1. Both are covered with forest, and are located immediately south of the bridge over the Damariscotta River.

DIRECTIONS: Follow U. S. Route 1 to where it crosses the Damariscotta River. Middens are immediately S of bridge, on either side of the river (Figure 38).

PUBLIC USE: The grounds upon which these sites are located are not accessible to the public. The sites can be viewed from U. S. Route 1.

FOR ADDITIONAL INFORMATION: Contact: Bureau of Parks and Recreation, State House Station 22, Augusta, ME 04333, 207-289-2211. **Read:** (1) Chadbourne, P. A. 1859. Oyster shell deposit in Damariscotta. Collections of the Maine Historical Society, vol. 6, pp. 347-351. (2) Snow, Dean R. 1972. Rising sea level and prehistoric cultural ecology in northern New England. American Antiquity, vol. 37, pp. 211-221. (3) Sanger, David, and Mary Jo (Elson) Sanger. 1986. Boom and bust on the river: The story of the Damariscotta oyster shell heaps. Archaeology of Eastern North America, vol. 14, pp. 65-78.

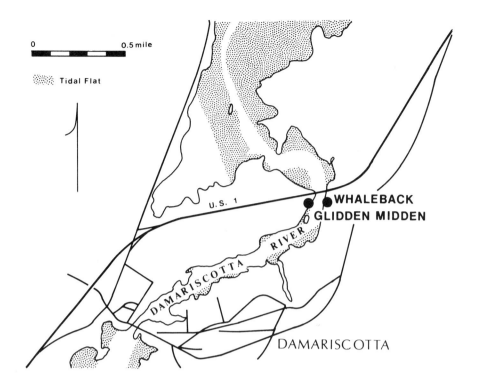

Figure 38. Location of Damariscotta Middens.

4. Nauset Marsh Site

Protohistoric Indian Settlement Site
Barnstable County, Massachusetts

"Indeed, the Cape was at first thickly settled by Indians on account of the abundance of oysters and other fish. We saw many traces of their occupancy . . . oysters, clams, cockles, and other shells, mingled with ashes and the bones of deer and other quadrupeds" (Henry David Thoreau, Cape Cod, 1914, p. 99).

When Samuel de Champlain explored the coast of Cape Cod in the summer of 1605, he located a village of the Nauset Indians encircling the shores of a bay he called Port de Mallebarre, today's Nauset Marsh. These Indians were practicing horticulture, but they also depended upon hunting and gathering for a significant part of their subsistence needs. Shellfish were among the resources they gathered, and shell middens were among the results of that activity. The Nauset did not produce any large middens around Nauset Marsh, but they did leave numerous small piles of shell in the vicinity of their village. Ecological conditions in and around the marsh are unfavorable to the development of high levels of shellfish productivity.

Indians often planted crops on "shell fields" to take advantage of the nutrients available from the shells. Whether or not the Nauset farmed their middens, Euro-American settlers on Cape Cod did just that. Consequently, the middens at Nauset Marsh are now all subsurface features. This site illustrates two important facts relevant to the formation and preservation of shell middens. (1) Shellfish gathering by Native Americans continued into the Historic Period, until either the resource was destroyed (because of changes in the aquatic environment or exploitation patterns) or the Indians were displaced. (2) Euro-Americans obscured surface evidence of middens in a variety of ways, one of which was by farming the "shell fields" themselves.

The Nauset Marsh Site is located on Cape Cod National Seashore and is administered by the National Park Service. Nauset Marsh can be viewed, or visited, from several points east of U. S. Route 6 in Eastham. Two interpretive signs at Skiff Hill overlook the marsh and relate particularly to the Nauset Indians.

DIRECTIONS: From the intersection of U. S. Route 6 and Massachusetts State Route 28 in Orleans, follow Route 6 N 1.5 mi. to Fort Hill Road, then go E 0.3 mi. to Fort Hill Trail. Skiff Hill interpretive signs overlooking Nauset Marsh are 0.25 mi. down this trail (Figure 39).

PUBLIC USE: Season and hours: The National Seashore grounds are open 6:00 AM-Midnight, daily. **Fees:** $3.00 per car, only for entrance to beaches, late June to Labor Day. **Recreational facilities:** Picnic areas, restrooms, trails, swimming, surfing, bicycling, horseback riding, fishing, hunting. **Handicapped facilities:** Many facilities at Cape Cod National Seashore are accessible to handicapped persons, including both visitor centers, Herring Cove

Beach and bathhouse, and the Buttonbush Trail — a rope guided nature trail with signs in large type and Braille. **Restrictions:** The disturbance or collecting of archeological resources, plants, or animals is prohibited. Pets must be on a 6' (or shorter) leash, and are not permitted in public buildings, picnic areas, protected beaches, or nature trails. See park regulations for additional restrictions and precautions.

EDUCATIONAL FACILITIES: Visitor centers: Two visitor centers are located in Cape Cod National Seashore: Salt Pond Visitor Center is on Route 6 in Eastham and Province Lands Visitor Center is on Race Point Road in Provincetown. The Salt Pond Visitor Center has an exhibit on the archeology of Cape Cod. **Visitor center hours:** Salt Pond Visitor Center —9:00 AM-4:30 PM daily, March through December; Closed January and February. Province Lands Visitor Center — 9:00 AM-4:30 PM daily, mid-April through November; Closed December through mid-April. Both visitor centers are open until 6:00 PM during July and August. When the visitor centers are closed, information is available at park headquarters in South Wellfleet and at Race Point Ranger Station in Provincetown. **Fees:** There is no charge for access to visitor centers. **Bookstore:** Educational publications are sold at both visitor centers and at park headquarters. **Trails:** Several self-guiding nature trails are located in the park. **Staff programs:** Park rangers provide guided walks, talks, and evening programs daily throughout the summer and on a reduced schedule in spring and from Labor Day through Columbus Day.

FOR ADDITIONAL INFORMATION: Contact: Superintendent, Cape Cod National Seashore, South Wellfleet, MA 02663, 617-349-3785. **Read:** (1) McManamon, Francis P. 1982. Prehistoric land use on outer Cape Cod. Journal of Field Archaeology, vol. 9, pp. 1-21. (2) McManamon, Francis P., and Christopher L. Borstel. 1982. The Archeology of Cape Cod National Seashore. Eastern National Parks and Monument Association. (3) McManamon, Francis P. (ed.), 1984, Chapters in the Archeology of Cape Cod. Boston: National Park Service. Two volumes.

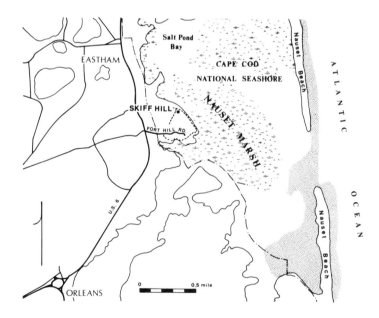

Figure 39. Location of Nauset Marsh Site.

5. Fort Shantok

Historic Indian Settlement Site
New London County, Connecticut

Fort Shantok preserves the location of the principal fort of the Mohegan-Pequot Indians during the early period of the European colonization of Connecticut. This fort was located upon a ridge immediately west of, and overlooking, the Thames River. Uncas, principal sachem of the Mohegans from 1637 until 1682 or 1683, is the Indian leader most closely associated with this fort. Many conflicts took place at Fort Shantok between the Mohegans and their adversaries, but the site and its environs was also used for habitation. In 1650, Jonathan Brewster established a trading post on the east side of the river, thereby focusing additional activity on the area.

Fort Shantok is included in this book as a representative example of those sites that document the gathering of shellfish by Native American populations into the Historic Period. Although no raised middens are visible at this site, small shell middens did occur at Fort Shantok and some reportedly aboriginal shell remains can still be seen at the foot of the ridge, alongside the river by the railroad tracks. Remnants of the fort's stone foundation can also be seen at the north end of the fort site.

This site is maintained today as Fort Shantok State Park. The park includes several interpretive signs and commemorative plaques. The partly stockaded "Ye Olde Mohegan Burial Ground" is located adjacent to (and is accessible from) the park. This cemetery is still used by the Mohegan-Pequot community.

DIRECTIONS: Exit Interstate 395 (Connecticut Turnpike) at Exit 79A, go E 0.5 mi. to Connecticut Route 32, then N on Route 32 0.2 mi. to Fort Shantok Rd., then E on Fort Shantok Rd. 0.8 mi. to Fort Shantok State Park on NE side of road (Figure 40).

PUBLIC USE: Season and hours: Grounds are open 8:00 AM-Sunset, daily. Fees: $1.00 parking charge holidays and weekends. **Recreational facilities:** Picnic areas, restrooms, camping, fishing, ice skating, ball fields. **Restrictions:** Dogs must be on leash at all times. Keg beer prohibited.

FOR ADDITIONAL INFORMATION: Contact: Manager, Fort Shantok State Park, Uncasville, CT 06382, 203-848-9876. **Read:** Salwen, Bert. 1966. European trade goods and the chronology of the Fort Shantok Site. Archaeological Society of Connecticut, Bulletin 34, pp. 5-39.

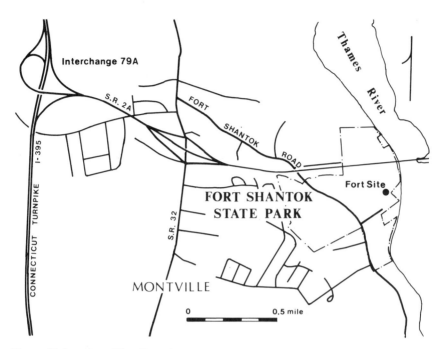

Figure 40. Location of Fort Shantok.

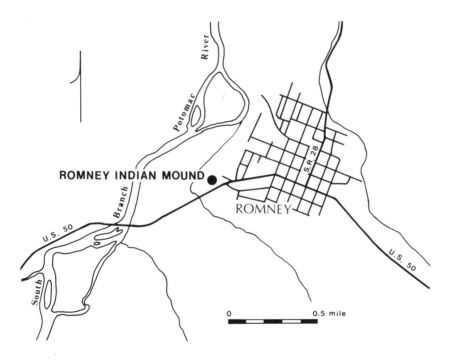

Figure 41. Location of Romney Mound.

70

6. Romney Indian Mound

Woodland Burial Mound
Romney, Hampshire County, West Virginia

The Romney Indian Mound is located in Indian Mound Cemetery, situated on a bluff about 150' above the valley of the South Branch of the Potomac River on the southwest side of Romney, in Indian Mound Cemetery (Figure 16). This mound is about 7' high; it has never been excavated, but it is considered to be late Woodland in age, dating from between A.D. 500-1000. The mound lies in a grove of several large trees southwest of the cemetery road, about 75 yards inside the gate.

The Confederate Monument located in this cemetery was erected by the Ladies of the Confederate Memorial Association and dedicated on September 26, 1867. This is considered one of the first monuments to southern soldiers who died in the American Civil War and documents one of the earliest Memorial Day services.

An historical marker commemorating the Indian Mound is located along the north side of U. S. Route 50 (Main Street) immediately southwest of the entrance to the cemetery.

DIRECTIONS: Follow U. S. Route 50 W 0.45 mi. from the West Virginia Route 28/U. S. 50 intersection, or E 0.7 mi. from the bridge over the Potomac River, to an unnamed road on the N side of U. S. 50 leading to Indian Mound Cemetery. Follow this unnamed road 0.1 mi. to cemetery. Indian Mound is about 75 yards inside cemetery, ahead, to left (Figure 41).

PUBLIC USE: Season and hours: Indian Mound Cemetery is open year round.

FOR ADDITIONAL INFORMATION: Contact: Archeologist, West Virginia Department of Culture and History, The Cultural Center, Capitol Complex, Charleston, WV 25305, 304-348-0240.

7. Hyer Mound

Woodland Burial Mound
Randolph County, West Virginia

The Hyer Mound is located on the top of a low ridge in the upper Tygart Valley of eastern West Virginia. The crest of this ridge is about 30' above, and immediately southeast of, Elkwater Fork near where that stream enters Tygart Valley River. Twenty burials were found in or beneath the mound when it was excavated by the West Virginia Geological Survey in 1963. Seven of the burials were partially covered with waterworn stones. One skeleton had been cremated, three corpses appeared to have been buried in the flesh, and the remaining skeletons represented bundle burials. The mound was constructed of sandy clay, probably between about A.D. 500-1000. Following excavation, the mound was restored to its original dimensions (5' high, 40' × 44' in diameter at the base).

Hyer Mound is located on private property, and trespassing is strictly prohibited. However, the mound is only about 75 yards south of U. S. Route 219, on a ridge in a pasture between the road and the old Hyer log cabin, and can be seen easily from the highway. In fact, the panoramic view of this mound and its environs from U. S. 219 provides an unusually clear view of the physical setting typical of many small, upland burial mounds af the Woodland Period.

DIRECTIONS: Hyer Mound lies about 75 yards S of U. S. Route 219, 9 mi. S of Huttonsville and 5.1 mi. N of the West Virginia Route 15/U. S. Route 219 intersection in Valley Head (Figure 42).

PUBLIC USE: Restrictions: This mound is located on private property. Trespassing is strictly prohibited.

FOR ADDITIONAL INFORMATION: Contact: Archeologist, West Virginia Department of Culture and History, The Cultural Center, Capitol Complex, Charleston, WV 25305, 304-348-0240. **Read:** Broyles, Bettye J. 1964. (Abstract) Mounds in Randolph County, West Virginia. Eastern States Archeological Federation Bulletin, vol. 23, p. 9.

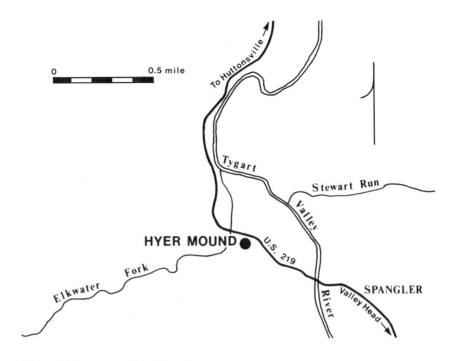

Figure 42. Location of Hyer Mound.

8. Town Creek Mound

Mississippian Ceremonial Center
Montgomery County, North Carolina

Town Creek Indian Mound State Historic Site is a reconstructed ceremonial center of Indians of the Mississippian Pee Dee Culture. Town Creek
was in use as a ceremonial center between about A.D. 1450 and 1650, and
lies on the northeastern frontier of Late Mississippian platform mound
building activity.

Archeological excavations have been carried out at Town Creek since
1937 under the direction of Dr. Joeffre L. Coe with the support of the
Research Laboratories of Anthropology at the University of North Carolina.
As a result of this long period of investigation, abundant information is
available with which to interpret the prehistory of the site. Much of the
information gained from 50 years of archeological investigation at the site
has been converted into museum exhibits and site reconstructions by
which visitors can gain an unusually comprehensive and integrated understanding of the patterns and functions of the Pee Dee people, and can see
and experience some of the benefits of publicly supported archeology.

The site reconstruction contains several buildings and other structures in the same pattern that they occurred when the ceremonial center
was in use. The central feature is the platform mound, containing a
wooden-staired earthen ramp and surmounted by a reconstructed
thatched-roof temple. Near the platform mound is a circular mortuary
house in which is depicted a funeral ceremony interring a bundle burial. At
the foot of the ramp leading to the top of the platform mound is the "square
ground" — the sacred surface upon which dwelt the *Talwa,* the sacred soul
of the tribe. Adjacent to the square ground a game pole, sporting the skull
of a bear at the top, rises upward some 40'. Surrounding these structures is
a palisade — the smallest of four that once existed at the site — with two
gates, each passing beneath a protective tower.

The area within the palisade at Town Creek was for ceremonial, not
residential, use. It was here that the honored dead were taken to be prepared for burial and, eventually, interred. Athletic contests between teams
from different villages took place in the area adjacent to the game pole. The
most important ceremony was the *Busk* or *Green Corn Dance,* a celebra-
tion that lasted eight days and marked the annual renewal of many features
of Pee Dee life. At the end of the *Busk,* Indians obtained embers from a
sacred fire, newly-made in the temple, to take back to their villages. New
fires were made from these embers. Since all fires in all the villages were
made from embers of the same sacred fire in the Town Creek temple, the
Pee Dee — and other people of Mississippian culture — called themselves
"people of one fire."

DIRECTIONS: From intersection of North Carolina routes 73 and 731 in Mount Gilead, follow Route 731 E 4.0 mi., then go S on Montgomery County Road 1542 1.1 mi. to Town Creek Indian Mound State Historic Site entrance on E side of road. From U. S. 220 at Ellerbe, go W on North Carolina State Route 73 approximately 13 mi., then N on Richmond County Road 1160 (which becomes Montgomery County Road 1542) 2.1 mi. to site entrance (Figure 43).

PUBLIC USE: Season and hours: The grounds are open 9:00 AM-5:00 PM, Monday through Saturday, 1:00-5:00 PM, Sunday, April 1 through October 31; 10:00 AM-4:00 PM, Tuesday through Saturday, 1:00-4:00 PM, Sunday, closed Monday, November 1 through March 31. Hours may vary. **Fees:** None. **Food Service:** Snacks and drinks may be purchased. **Recreational facilities:** Picnic area, restrooms, foot trail. **Handicapped facilities:** Most of the site's public areas are accessible by wheelchair.

EDUCATIONAL FACILITIES: Museum: The museum offers a variety of exhibits on the Town Creek Site and North Carolina archeology generally. An 18 minute narrated slide program provides an introduction to the site and its builders. Complementing this introduction are exhibits on pottery, urn burials, the *Busk,* and ceremonial life, all of which are given chronological context by an overview of North Carolina prehistory. A photo essay on excavation activity at Town Creek, and a photomosaic of the excavation plan, provide additional insight into the archeology of the site. **Museum hours:** Same as grounds hours (above). **Fees:** None. **Bookstore:** A modest selection of books and other educational matter, especially for school children, is offered for sale. **Special group activities:** The site staff will provide guided tours and hands-on activities for school groups, but advance reservations are necessary and should be made *at least* two weeks before the planned visit.

FOR ADDITIONAL INFORMATION: Contact: Site Manager, Town Creek Indian Mound State Historic Site, Route 3, Box 50, Mt. Gilead, NC 27306, 919-439-6802. **Read:** South, Stanley. 1973. The temple at Town Creek Mound State Historic Site, North Carolina. The Institute of Archeology and Anthropology — The University of South Carolina, Notebook, vol. 5, pp. 145-171.

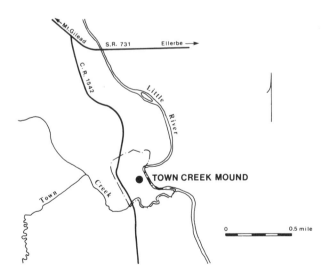

Figure 43. Location of Town Creek Site.

75

9. Nikwasi Mound

Mississippian Platform Mound
Franklin, Macon County, North Carolina

Nikwasi Mound is representative of a class of relatively small conical platform mounds built by Late Mississippian Indians in the Appalachian Summit Region of Georgia, North Carolina, South Carolina and Tennessee (Figure 24A). This mound is generally circular with a graded ascent on one side, and is about 15' high. Nikwasi is located on the floodplain of the Little Tennessee River, about 0.1 mile west of the present course of that river, and is maintained as greenspace by the City of Franklin.

This mound was standing when people of the Qualla Phase, ancestors of the historic Cherokee, appeared in and around the Appalachian Summit. Like other pre-existing mounds of the region, however, it became integrated into Cherokee lifeways and folklore. Nikwasi, or Nequassee, was one of the Cherokee Middle settlements. As was common practice among the Cherokee, the townhouse was built on the top of the mound so that it would be elevated for symbolic and practical reasons. James Mooney and Charles Hudson recount some elements of Cherokee mythology associated with this mound (see below, For Additional Information).

In 1732, the eccentric Scottish adventurer, Sir Alexander Cuming, spoke in the Nequassee townhouse to assembled leaders from Cherokee settlements on both sides of the Great Smoky Mountains. He invited six to accompany him to London, where they were treated as celebreties. These unofficial representatives of the Cherokee negotiated and signed a trade and mutual defense treaty with the British, the Treaty of 1730, which — although illegal — became the basis of subsequent relations between the Cherokee and the Carolina colonists. In 1760 the Cherokee rebelled against Carolinian noncompliance with the treaty. The following spring, British soldiers marched on the Middle settlements, burning towns, destroying fields of new corn, and felling peach orchards. At dawn, on June 11 they entered Nequassee to find it abandoned. They tore down the homes but spared the townhouse on the mound, which they converted to a hospital for wounded British troops. As a result of this punitive expedition, the Middle Cherokee fled to the Overhill settlements west of the Great Smoky Mountains.

DIRECTIONS: Follow North Carolina State Route 28 E 0.6 mi. from Macon County Courthouse to Nikwasi Mound along N side of road. Parking is available on E or W side of mound.

FOR ADDITIONAL INFORMATION: Read: (1) Mooney, James. 1900. Myths of the Cherokee. Bureau of American Ethnology, 19th Annual Report (see pp. 395-6, 477). (2) Hudson, Charles. 1976. The Southeastern Indians. Knoxville: University of Tennessee Press (see pp. 169-71).

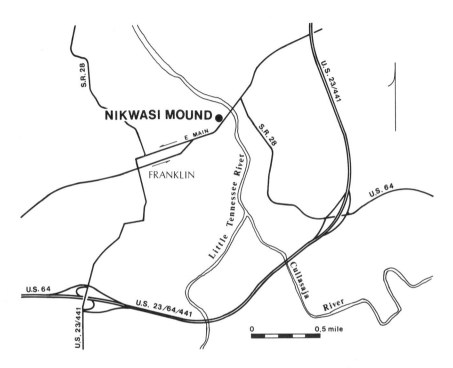

Figure 44. Location of Nikwasi Mound.

10. Sewee Shell Ring

Late Archaic Shell Ring
Charleston County, South Carolina

Sewee Shell Ring, also known locally as the "Spanish Fort," is one of the northernmost shell rings. A large part of this feature has been destroyed by the removal of shells in the past for road surfacing and other uses. The Sewee Ring is presently between a few feet to about 10' in height, and more than 100' across. The ring is covered with trees and shrubs which help to stabilize and preserve the feature.

The Sewee Shell Ring is on the southeastern edge of Francis Marion National Forest, immediately northwest of the Atlantic Intracoastal Waterway, where the oak-pine forest meets the tidal marsh. This site is reached by a 5-10 minute walk along a level, one-quarter mile long foot trail through the coastal forest. The site is fenced along its north side to prevent access by motor vehicles, but the fence is offset to allow foot traffic to pass.

DIRECTIONS: Approximately 21 mi. N of Charleston, exit U. S. Route 17 onto South Carolina Route 432, go 3.8 mi. S (if southbound) or 2.3 mi. N (if northbound) on Route 432 to unpaved Forest Road 243 (Salt Pond Road), then go 0.3 mi. SE on Road 243 to welded tubular steel barricade on SW (right) side of road. Trail (0.5 mi. round trip) to shell ring begins at barricade (Figure 45).

PUBLIC USE: Season and hours: Open 24 hours each day. **Fees:** None. **Recreational facilities:** None at site. Picnic areas, restrooms, camping, hiking, boating, fishing, and birding are available elsewhere in Francis Marion National Forest and Cape Romain National Wildlife Refuge. **Restrictions:** Disturbance or removal of archeological resources is strictly prohibited.

FOR ADDITIONAL INFORMATION: Contact: District Ranger, Wambaw Ranger District, Francis Marion National Forest, P. O. Box 788, McClellanville, SC 29458, 803-887-3311.

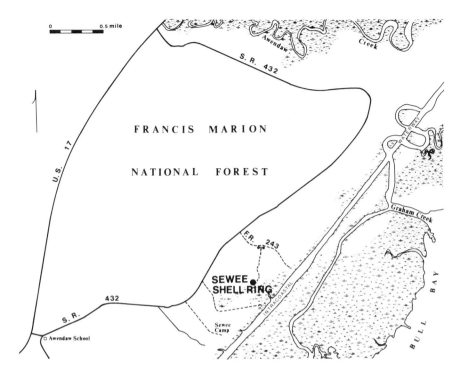

Figure 45. Location of Sewee Shell Ring.

11. Spanish Mount

Late Archaic Shell Midden
Charleston County, South Carolina

Spanish Mount, built primarily of oyster shells, is about 8' high and is presently covered with small trees and dense shrubs. The mound is located on the south tip of a small peninsula that projects into the marshy tidal flats along Scott Creek. Erosion by the tide-induced rise and fall of Scott Creek is eroding the southeast face of Spanish Mount. This circumstance affords the visitor the opportunity of seeing one way in which natural processes can alter or destroy prehistoric human works. The exposed southeast face of eroding Spanish Mount also presents a representative cross-sectional view of the structure of shell mounds. This mound is believed to have been built about 4,000 years ago by Indians of the Late Archaic Period that lived on Edisto Island and exploited the shellfish resources that occurred along the coast.

Spanish Mount is located in the southwestern part of Edisto Beach State Park. The site can be reached only by a foot trail 2 miles in length (4 miles round trip). This peaceful, level trail passes through a lowland coastal evergreen forest dominated by pine, palmetto, and oaks draped with Spanish Moss. One branch of the trail crosses a wooden bridge built above an arm of the park's salt marsh. Yaupon, the plant from which the *Black Drink* of the southeastern Indians was made, can be seen growing at several places along this trail. At the mound the trail splits into two branches, one leading up to the top of the feature and the other leading around its base. Climbing on and removing shells from the mound accelerates its destruction and should be avoided.

DIRECTIONS: From U. S. Route 17 about 25 mi. SW of Charleston, go 21 mi. S on South Carolina Route 174 to unnamed park road on S side of road (0.1 mi. S of park entrance), then go 0.2 mi. W on unnamed park road to Indian Mound Trail parking area immediately N of road. The trail to the mound is ca. 4 mi. in length, round trip (Figure 46).

PUBLIC USE: Season and hours: The park is open daily throughout the year; Indian Mound Trail is open to use daily from sunrise to sunset. **Fees:** None. **Recreational facilities:** Picnic areas, restrooms, hiking, camping, beachcombing, boating.

EDUCATIONAL FACILITIES: Trail: Several species of shrubs and trees are identified along parts of the 4 mi. (round trip) Indian Mound Trail. Some additional information about the natural history of this trail is contained in the *Edisto Beach State Park* brochure.

FOR ADDITIONAL INFORMATION: Contact: Michael Foley, Chief Historian, South Carolina Department of Parks, Recreation and Tourism, P. O. Box 110, Columbia, SC 29201, 803-758-3622.

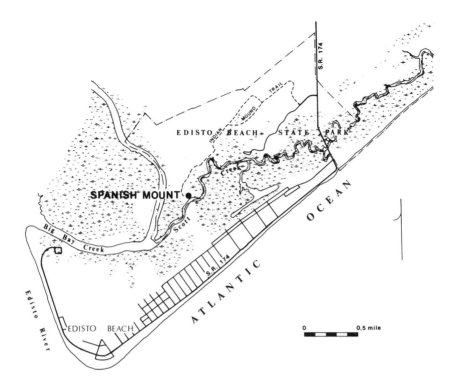

Figure 46. Location of Spanish Mount.

12. Sea Pines Shell Ring

Late Archaic Shell Ring
Beaufort County, South Carolina

The Sea Pines Shell Ring is located on the southern part of Hilton Head Island in the Sea Pines Plantation Forest Reserve, a publicly accessible property of the privately owned Sea Pines Plantation. This ring can be reached only on foot by a short nature trail approximately 0.5 mile in length, round trip.

This ring is composed primarily of oyster shell. The ring is about 150' in diameter, 3' in height, and dates to about 3,500 years ago.

DIRECTIONS: Follow U. S. Route 278 onto Hilton Head Island and continue to Sea Pines Circle, then go 0.5 mi. S on Greenwood Drive to Sea Pines Forest Preserve West Entrance on E. To reach East Entrance of Preserve, continue S on Greenwood Dr. 0.1 mi., then go S on Tupelo Rd. 0.2 mi. to Lawton Lane, then NE on Lawton Lane 0.05 mi. to East Entrance. Parking is available inside both West and East entrances (Figure 47).

PUBLIC USE: Season and hours: The Forest Preserve is open from sunrise to sunset, daily. **Fees:** $3.00 per car admission to Sea Pines Plantation; includes admission to Forest Preserve. **Restrictions:** Smoking is not permitted in the Preserve.

FOR ADDITIONAL INFORMATION: Contact: Sea Pines Security Office, 18 Greenwood Dr., Hilton Head, SC 29938, 803-671-7170.

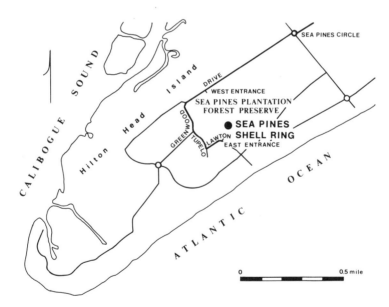

Figure 47. Location of Sea Pines Shell Ring.

13. Fort Watson Mound

Mississippian Platform Mound
Clarendon County, South Carolina

This mound is located in the Bluff Unit of the Santee National Wildlife Refuge but is administered by the South Carolina Department of Parks, Recreation and Tourism through the adjacent Santee State Park. The mound is the focal point of a small park located on the north side of Lake Marion, an artificial reservoir on the Santee River. A parking area is located about 50 yards from the mound. The mound is now covered with trees and shrubs, but wooden stairs provide access to the top of the feature. Park benches overlook Lake Marion, and the Wrights Bluff Nature Trail can be accessed at this park. In a protected bay just beyond the mound is a picturesque grove of young bald cypress trees draped with Spanish Moss.

Fort Watson (or Santee) Mound is a Late Mississippian platform mound, representative of mounds on the eastern fringes of the Late Mississippian culture area. During the Revolutionary War, British forces built a stockade on top of this mound as one of a chain of forts through the Southeast. This fort, Fort Watson, controlled movements on the Santee River and the Charleston-Camden Road. In mid-April, 1781, Revolutionary soldiers under the command of General Francis Marion surrounded the fort. A log tower was built under the direction of Major Hezekiah Mahan so that the American soldiers could more effectively fire down upon the fort. Subsequently, the walls of Fort Watson were undermined and the garrison surrendered on April 23, 1781.

DIRECTIONS: Exit Interstate Highway 95 at Exit 102, go N on combined U. S. Routes 15/301 for 0.3 mi., then W on unnamed U. S. Wildlife Refuge Road for 1.0 mi. to mound parking area on W side of road (Figure 48).

PUBLIC USE: Season and hours: The mound site is open daily, sunrise to sunset. **Fees:** None. **Recreational facilities:** Picnic area, restrooms, hiking, birding, boating, fishing, hunting (seasonal) on the refuge; additional facilities available in Santee State Park. **Restrictions:** Walking on the mound, other than on the wooden stairway, is prohibited.

FOR ADDITIONAL INFORMATION: Contact: Michael Foley, Chief Historian, South Carolina Department of Parks, Recreation and Tourism, P. O. Box 110, Columbia, SC 27201, 803-758-3622 *or* Refuge Manager, Santee National Wildlife Refuge, Route 2, Box 66, Summerton, SC 29148, 803-478-2217.

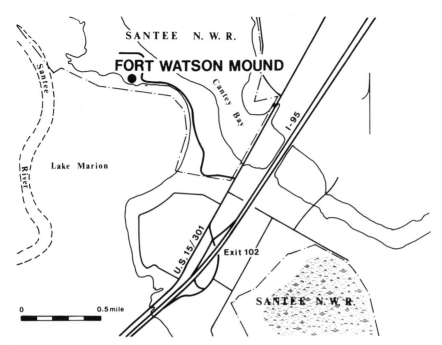

Figure 48. Location of Fort Watson Mound.

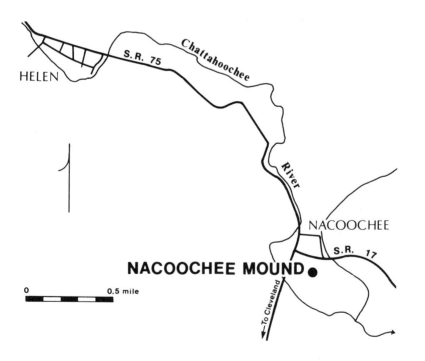

Figure 49. Location of Nacoochee Mound.

14. Nacoochee Mound

Mississippian Platform Mound
White County, Georgia

Nacoochee Mound, also known as the Hardman Mound, is situated on the floodplain of the upper Chattahoochee River in the Appalachian Mountains of northeastern Georgia. This elliptical mound was described in 1873 as being 20' high and 190' × 150' at the base. Excavations in 1915 by the Heye Foundation revealed that the mound had been enlarged at least four times and contained about 75 burials. Pottery shards suggested that Nacoochee was built by people of the Lamar culture. Later, this was the site of a Cherokee village (Nae-oche), still occupied when William Bartram passed through the region in 1776.

Nacoochee, now grass-covered with a gazebo on top, is in a farm pasture on private property. The site is fenced and is not accessible to the public, but the mound can be seen easily from public highways.

DIRECTIONS: Follow Georgia State Route 75 N 8 mi. from the White County courthouse in Cleveland, or S 2 mi. from the business district in Helen. The mound is located in the pasture E of Route 75, immediately SE of the intersection of Georgia Routes 17/75 (Figure 49).

PUBLIC USE: Restrictions: This mound is located on private property, which is posted. Trespassing is not permitted.

FOR ADDITIONAL INFORMATION: Contact: Manager, Georgia Master Site File, Department of Anthropology, University of Georgia, Athens, GA 30602. **Read:** (1) Heye, George G., F. W. Hodge, and George H. Pepper. 1918. The Nacoochee Mound in Georgia. Contributions, Museum of the American Indian, Heye Foundation, vol. 4, no. 3. (2) Wauchope, Robert. 1966. Archaeological Survey of Northern Georgia, with a Test of some Cultural Hypotheses. Memoirs of the Society for American Archaeology, no. 21.

15. Fort Mountain Stone Wall

Late Woodland Stone Feature
Murray County, Georgia

This stone wall zig-zags for more than 900' in a generally east-west direction across Fort Mountain, one of the highest peaks in the Cohutta Mountains of northwest Georgia. Presently, most of the wall is between 2'-3' in height, although some higher sections are about 7' high (Figure 15). The wall was probably higher when first built. Twenty nine circular pits several feet in diameter and spaced about 30' apart are located along the course of the wall. A single gap in the wall is interpreted as a gateway. The wall runs from precipice to precipice across Fort Mountain, separating the small, gently sloping summit area from the lower ridge to the south.

Fort Mountain takes its name from this stone wall which has been considered by some interpreters to have been a defensive structure. The actual function, the age, and the builders of the wall, however, are not known, and a rich body of Indian and American folklore, scientific opinion, and romantic musing has developed around the uncertainty. No diagnostic artifacts have been found at or near the wall, so virtually no material evidence other than the wall itself is available with which to interpret the feature. Most archeologists agree that the wall was built by Indians, probably Late Woodland Indians, but nobody knows for certain why.

The stone wall is well placed strategically for a defensive or isolating structure, extending as it does completely across the only gentle slope leading to the peak of Fort Mountain. Some archeologists have considered that the wall might have been built for some religious or other ceremonial function, perhaps a calenderic device for determining the summer (solar) and winter (lunar) solstices and other important astronomical events. Archaeoastronomer John W. Burgess, one proponent of the calenderic function for the stone wall, has proposed recently that the wall might also represent a map of the territory of its builders. The wall dips and rises in a pattern that corresponds closely to the changing elevation of the horizon as viewed nearly perpendicular to the wall.

The stone wall is reached on foot by Old Fort Loop Trail. This trail is 1.3 miles long and well marked. The wall lies only about 900' from the trail head, however, so it is not necessary to walk the entire trail to see the stone feature. Take the left branch of the trail, at the trail head, for the most direct route to the wall.

DIRECTIONS: From Chatsworth, take Georgia Route 52 E 7.5 mi. to Fort Mountain State Park entrance, enter park and continue W 2.25 mi. to Fort Loop parking area (Figure 50).

PUBLIC USE: Season and hours: Open daily throughout the year, 7:00 AM-10:00 PM. **Fees:** None to visit stone wall. **Recreational facilities:** Picnic areas, restrooms, camping, cottages, hiking, swimming, fishing, boating. **Restrictions:** Pets must be on leash no greater than 6′ in length and accompanied by owner at all times.

EDUCATIONAL FACILITIES: Trail: Three interpretive signs along Old Fort Loop Trail, 1.3 mi. in length, provide information about the stone wall.

FOR ADDITIONAL INFORMATION: Contact: Superintendent, Fort Mountain State Park, Route 7, Box 1K, Chatsworth, GA 30705, 404-695-2621. **Read:** Wauchope, Robert. 1966. Archaeological Survey of Northern Georgia with a Test of some Cultural Hypotheses. Memoirs of the Society for American Archaeology, no. 21.

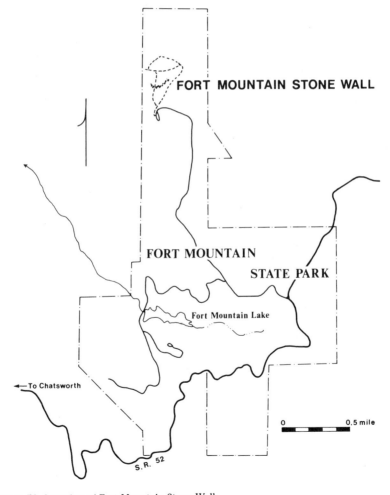

Figure 50. Location of Fort Mountain Stone Wall.

16. Etowah Mounds

Mississippian Ceremonial Center
Bartow County, Georgia

The Etowah mounds mark the location of the most important political and religious center in the Etowah Valley between about A.D. 1000 and 1500. Here was located a town of 1,000-2,000 or more people along with the religious and political leaders of the region. The town centered upon the large temple mound and two smaller platform mounds located north of the Etowah River (Figure 22). The large mound (Mound A) apparently supported structures used by the political and religious leaders, whereas the smaller mound to the southwest (Mound C) was the mortuary mound, site of the charnel house and numerous burials. East of the large mound was the plaza, beyond which were four small, conical mounds. The town was bordered on the south by the Etowah River, and to the north, east, and west by a palisade and ditch. Houses for residents were built inside the protective ditch-palisade-river barriers.

The large temple mound (Mound A) is about 60' high and about 335' × 395' at the base. This mound contained two distinct platform levels. Cyrus Thomas wrote, in 1894, "This is truly a grand and remarkable structure, being exceeded in size in the United States. . .only by the great Cahokia mound. . .It (Etowah Mound A) . . .exceeds slightly in volume the entire wall of Fort Ancient, in Ohio. . ." (pp. 300-1). A straight ramp, typical of those on Mississippian platform mounds, was centered on the east side. A wider, curving ramp was constructed on the south side and southwest corner of the mound during the 19th Century by farmers to enable them to reach the top.

The mortuary mound (Mound C) was excavated in the 1880s by the Bureau of (American) Ethnology, in the 1920s by the Phillips Academy of Andover, Massachusetts, and on different occasions — since 1953 — by the Georgia Historical Commission. Several hundred burials have been recovered from within or around the base of this mound. Some burials were extended in-the-flesh burials, some of which were buried in stone tombs. Bundle burials and cremations were also represented. Grave goods associated with many of these burials were extremely rich and elaborate. Well represented were objects related to the Southern Ceremonial Complex and fine stone carvings, perhaps the most famous of which are two figures of humans carved in marble. Excavations of the village site have also been carried out. As a result of the relatively large number of investigations carried out at Etowah, many technical descriptive, analytical, and interpretive papers have been written about this mound group.

When the Reverend Elias Cornelius, the first American chronicler of the Etowah mounds, visited the site in 1817 he found the mounds densely vegetated and difficult to comprehend visually. Eight Cherokee chiefs had taken Cornelius to the site. "I had scarcely proceeded 200 yards when, through the thick forest trees, a stupendous pile met the eye... Its top...was so completely covered with weeds, bushes, and trees of most luxurient growth that I could not examine it as well as I wished." In the years following Cornelius's visit, the area around the mounds was cleared and farmed. The slopes of the lower mounds were cultivated, as were the tops of the high platform mounds. Today, the slopes of the large mounds are relatively free of tree growth, and visitors to Etowah Mounds State Historic Site have no difficulty comprehending the size and relationship among the major features of this once-prominent settlement site. The view from the top of the large mound is especially impressive and well worth the climb to the top.

DIRECTIONS: Exit Interstate 75 at Exit 124 onto Georgia State Routes 61/113, follow Georgia 61/113 through downtown Cartersville onto Etowah Dr., continue SW on Etowah Dr. 2.7 mi. to Etowah Mounds State Historic Site on S side of road (Figure 51).

PUBLIC USE: Season and hours: Grounds are open 9:00 AM-5:00 PM, Tuesday through Saturday; 2:00-5:30 PM, Sunday. Closed Mondays (except legal state or federal holidays), Thanksgiving, and Christmas. **Fees:** Adults (13 years and above) $1.50, children (6-12) $.75, children less than 6 years of age admitted free. Group rates for 15 or more are available. **Recreational facilities:** Picnic area, restrooms.

EDUCATIONAL FACILITIES: Museum: The Etowah Museum exhibits provide an overview of the archeology of the Etowah region, but focus on the period between A.D. 1000-1500. Of special interest are exhibits depicting the richness of grave goods and the extent of interregional trade. **Museum hours:** Same as grounds hours (above). **Fees:** Grounds entry fee includes admission to museum. **Bookstore:** The museum offers for sale a modest selection of books and other educational materials. **Special events:** The Site sponsors Indian Skills Day in Spring and Fall, a Summer Solstice Program on or near June 21, and an Artifacts Identification Day once a year. Contact the Site for exact dates of these activities.

FOR ADDITIONAL INFORMATION: Contact: Superintendent, Etowah Mounds State Historic Site, Route 2, Cartersville, GA 30120, 404-382-2704. **Read:** (1) Thomas, Cyrus. 1894. Report on the Mound Explorations of the Bureau of Ethnology, Bureau of Ethnology, 12th Annual Report (see pp. 292-311). (2) Wauchope, Robert. 1966. Archaeological Survey of Northern Georgia, with a Test of some Cultural Hypotheses. Memoirs of the Society for American Archaeology, no. 21. (3) Moorehead, Warren K. 1932. Etowah Papers. New Haven: Yale University Press.

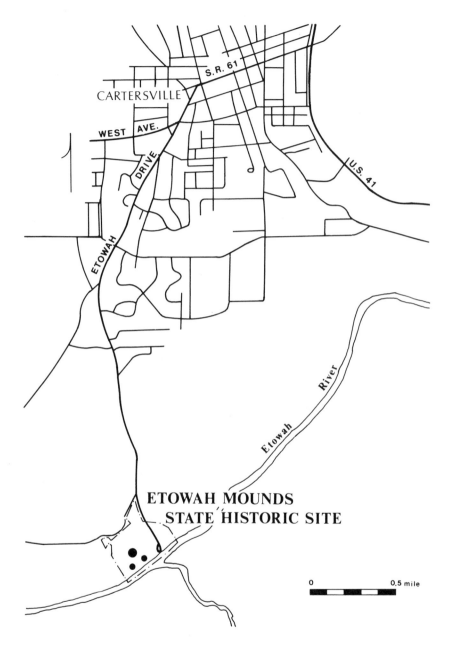

Figure 51. Location of Etowah Ceremonial Center.

17. Botanical Garden Mounds

Woodland Stone Mounds
Clarke County, Georgia

A cluster of small, conical stone mounds, or cairns, tentatively considered to be of Middle Woodland age, was recently discovered on the grounds of the State Botanical Garden of Georgia. At least 30 mounds have been identified to date, the largest measuring approximately 3' in height and 10' in diameter. The mounds are spread across about 2 acres of hilltop overlooking the Middle Oconee River. Clusters of small stone mounds often identify sites of multiple Indian burials.

The Botanical Garden mounds will be opened to public visitation in 1987, and will be the featured attraction of a self-guided trail interpreting the use of the Botanical Garden region by Native Americans.

DIRECTIONS: From combined U. S. Routes 129/441 on the S side of Athens, follow South Milledge Avenue S 1.1 mi. to The State Botanical Garden of Georgia, then go 0.7 mi. to conservatory and visitor center parking areas (Figure 52).

PUBLIC USE: Season and hours: The grounds of the Botanical Garden are open daily, 8:00 AM-Sunset. **Fees:** None. **Recreational facilities:** Five miles of marked trails wind through the Botanical Garden.

EDUCATIONAL FACILITIES: Conservatory: The conservatory and visitor center combines exhibits of fine art and botanic specimens. **Conservatory hours:** The conservatory and visitor center is open 9:00 AM-4:30 PM, Monday through Saturday; 11:30 AM-4:30 PM, Sunday. **Bookstore:** A selection of books, other educational materials, and gifts is available in the Conservatory gift shop. **Trails:** Flora is identified along some trails. A guidebook for use along the trail interpreting the Native American use of the region soon will be available. **Special group activities:** Group tours can be arranged through the education office. Please make arrangements *at least* 2 weeks in advance.

FOR ADDITIONAL INFORMATION: Contact: Education Office, The State Botanical Garden of Georgia, The University of Georgia, 2450 S. Milledge Ave., Athens, GA 30605, 404-542-1244.

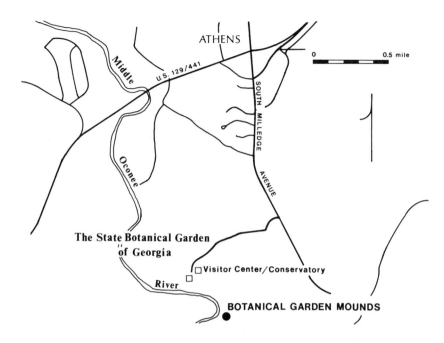

Figure 52. Location of Botanical Garden Mounds.

18. Rock Eagle Effigy Mound

Woodland Stone Effigy
Putnam County, Georgia

Formed entirely of milky quartz boulders, cobbles, and smaller stones, this effigy mound — in the likeness of a bird of prey or vulture — lies recumbent with outspread wings across a hilltop on the Piedmont of north central Georgia (Figure 14). The head of the bird is turned to the east. The wingspan is 120', and the distance from head to tail is 102'. The trunk of the body is up to 10' thick. A second effigy, almost identical to Rock Eagle, is located about 12 miles away.

Parts of the mound and surrounding area have been excavated on at least two occasions. The excavation of the mound itself provided information about the structure of the feature, but very few artifacts were recovered. Rock Eagle is considered by some archeologists to have been built about 1,500 years ago, based largely on pottery shards and the fact that other effigy mounds are considered that old. Some archeologists have suggested an age of some 5,000-6,000 years, based on a few artifacts recovered from beneath the mound during one of the excavations, but this age is not widely accepted. The mound is supposed to have had some ceremonial or religious function, being perhaps — in the opinion of some archeologists — the burial place of an important leader.

This mound is located on The Rock Eagle 4-H Center, a multi-purpose educational facility that is part of the University System of Georgia. The feature is fenced for security reasons, but is publicly accessible throughout the year. A stone tower has been built at the west end of the feature to permit visitors to see the effigy from above. (A wide angle lens is recommended for photographing the effigy from the tower; the standard 55-mm lens of most 35-mm cameras will not admit the entire effigy.)

DIRECTIONS: Enter Rock Eagle 4-H Center from combined U. S. Routes 129/441 7 mi. N of Eatonton, go 0.8 mi. W on Rock Eagle Rd., then W (right) at sign to Rock Eagle for 0.1 mi., then bear SW for 0.1 mi. to parking area for mound (Figure 53).

PUBLIC USE: Season and hours: Grounds are open 24 hours daily. **Fees:** None. **Recreational facilities:** Picnic area.

EDUCATIONAL FACILITIES: Publications: A brochure describing Rock Eagle effigy is available at no charge at the Center office. **Center program:** A resident environmental education program is available for elementary and middle school age children during the Fall and Spring months. During June, July, and August the Georgia 4-H Camping Program serves 5th-8th graders.

FOR ADDITIONAL INFORMATION: Contact: Rock Eagle 4-H Center, Eatonton, GA 31024, 404-485-2831.

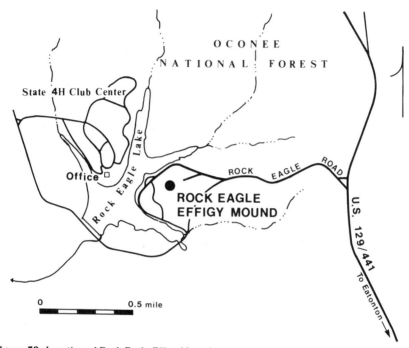

Figure 53. Location of Rock Eagle Effigy Mound.

19. Ocmulgee National Monument

Mississippian Ceremonial Center
Bibb County, Georgia

Ocmulgee National Monument, a unit of the National Park Service located immediately east of Macon, Georgia, is one of the most important and best interpreted publicly accessible mound sites in the Atlantic Coastal Region. Evidence of human presence at Ocmulgee spans some 11,000 years, extending from the Paleo-Indian Period to the Historic Period. The emphasis at Ocmulgee, however, is upon the mounds and other features built on the Macon Plateau and the nearby Ocmulgee River floodplain during the Mississippian Period. Visitors to Ocmulgee have the opportunity to see several archeological features unique to publicly accessible sites in the Atlantic coastal states.

About A.D. 900, the Mississippian settlement complex was established at Ocmulgee as an outlier of the main Middle Mississippi culture region located farther west. Here on the Macon Plateau overlooking the Ocmulgee River was built a large fortified town which contained more than 1,000 people at one time. Farming hamlets and isolated dwellings were scattered throughout the surrounding area, especially on the Ocmulgee River floodplain. At least seven mounds are known from within or near the main village area, including two known temple mounds, one burial mound, and four less well preserved mounds whose functions are known with less certainty (Figure 22). An unusual aspect of the Great Temple Mound is that part of it was sculpted out of the southern edge of the Macon Plateau; additional earthen material was added to elevate the platform (Figure 21). Religious and ceremonial structures and dwellings occurred within the town; significant among these were nine earthlodges, the largest of which has been restored and conditioned for public access (Figure 32). Bordering the town to the north and east are two parallel ditches, originally a series of large partially connected pits, some sections of which are lined with clay. These ditches might be borrow pits from which earth was taken to construct the mounds, or they may have served some defensive purpose.

The Macon Plateau village flourished until A.D. 1100, then declined. Two hundred years later, Indians of the Lamar Phase — a blend of Mississippian and Woodland culture — appeared in parts of the southeastern United States, including the Ocmulgee area. In fact, the Lamar Culture was recognized from evidence obtained at the Lamar Mounds and Village Site, a small detached unit of Ocmulgee National Monument located about 1.5 miles south of the Macon Plateau village. One of the two mounds at the Lamar Site is ascended by a unique spiral ramp. (The Lamar Site is not open to the public at this time.)

DIRECTIONS: Exit Interstate 16 at Exit 2 or 3. From Exit 2, go N on Gray St. about 0.1 mi., then E on Emery Highway 1.1 mi. to Ocmulgee National Monument on S side of road. From Exit 3, go N on U. S. Route 80 (Coliseum Dr.) 0.5 mi. to Emery Highway, then E on Emery Highway 0.7 mi. to the National Monument (Figure 54).

PUBLIC USE: Season and hours: The grounds are open 9:00 AM-5:00 PM daily; summer hours may be extended. Closed Christmas and New Years. **Fees:** $1.00 per person, ages 13-61, valid for seven days from date of purchase. Children less than 13, senior citizens 62 years or older, and residents who are blind or permanently disabled are admitted free. **Recreational facilities:** Picnic areas, trails. **Handicapped facilities:** Entrance ramp, restrooms; wheelchairs available. **Restrictions:** Climbing on the mounds, away from designated walkways and stairs, and departing from hiking trails are prohibited.

EDUCATIONAL FACILITIES: Museum: The visitor center houses a major museum of the archeology of the Macon Plateau and environs. A relief map of the region, including the mounds, is located near the entrance. Among the exhibits are depictions of the growth and structure of mounds, burials, Mississippian village and town organization, layout and use of earth lodges, elements of Mississippian culture, pottery, shellfish use, and the annual round of seasonal activities practiced by the Macon Plateau people. A 12-minute introductory film *People of the Macon Plateau* is shown every 30 minutes. Visitor-initiated videotapes about flint-knapping and hafting, and pottery making, are also available. A reconstructed earthlodge is situated about 800' southwest of the visitor center. This lodge was reconstructed, based on archeological evidence, over the original floor of the largest earthlodge found at Ocmulgee. The lodge can be entered; the environmentally-controlled interior is lighted and an audio program interprets the structure. **Museum hours:** Same as grounds hours. **Fees:** Grounds entry fee includes admission to museum. **Bookstore:** A book and gift shop is located in the visitor center; among the materials for sale are books about Indians, archeology, and natural history, and authentic Native American crafts. **Trails:** Several trails lead to the various mounds and other archeological features and natural areas. Interpretive signs and visitor-initiated audio programs are located at points of interest.

FOR ADDITIONAL INFORMATION: Contact: Superintendent, Ocmulgee National Monument, 1207 Emery Highway, Macon, GA 31201, 912-752-8257. **Read:** (1) Kelly, Arthur R. 1938. A Preliminary Report on Archaeological Explorations at Macon, Georgia. Bureau of American Ethnology, Bulletin 119, Anthropological Papers, no. 1. (2) Fairbanks, Charles H. 1946. The Macon Earthlodge. American Antiquity, vol. 12, pp. 94-108. (3) Fairbanks, Charles H. (with an introduction by Frank M. Setzler). 1956. Archeology of the Funeral Mound, Ocmulgee National Monument, Georgia. National Park Service, Archeological Research Series, no. 3.

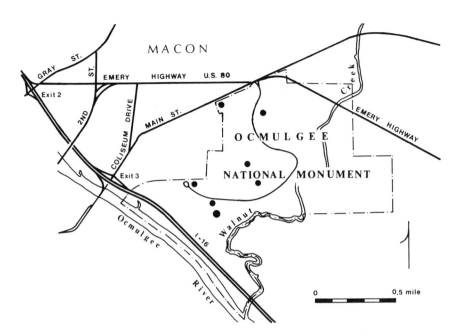

Figure 54. Location of Ocmulgee Ceremonial Center.

20. Kolomoki Mounds State Park

Woodland Ceremonial Center
Early County, Georgia

A complex of seven mounds dating mostly from the Middle and Late Woodland Period provides the archeological focus for Kolomoki Mounds State Park, a 1,293 acre facility given to the State of Georgia in 1938 by citizens of Early County. The mounds are in the park's archeological area and can be seen easily from the park road or visited on foot. Parking for visitors to the archeological area is located on the north side of the park road, almost directly opposite the group shelter. From here, a trail — approximately 1 mile long, round trip — leads to some of the mounds, including the Great Mound (Mound A, a platform mound). Steps ascend the top of the Great Mound. From this 56' high vantage point, it is a worth-while — perhaps irresistible — mental exercise to imagine the view and thoughts of the Indian leaders as they looked down upon the largest ceremonial complex and population center (containing perhaps 2,000 people) in the region in their time.

The history of occupation of the Kolomoki Site has been revised recently. According to the most recent interpretation, the earliest occupation of Kolomoki began about A.D. 400 by people of the Swift Creek Phase. By about A.D. 600, changes in the culture of people living at Kolomoki were sufficiently significant to have produced the Kolomoki form of Weeden Island culture which continued at the site until it was abandoned sometime after A.D. 900. The seven mounds within Kolomoki Park were built by people of the Kolomoki culture. The area around the mounds was again occupied by Indians during the 1500s, this time by people of the Lamar Phase.

The mound complex at Kolomoki includes one temple mound (A: Great Mound), two burial mounds (D, E), and four "ceremonial" mounds (B, C, F and H) whose specific functions are not known. A ridge of earth might have surrounded these mounds at one time, but — if so — it is lost. The Great Mound is 56' high and 200' × 325' at the base. Unlike typical platform mounds, Great Mound appears not to have had a ramp leading to its summit. Ascent and descent probably was made by steps set into one of the steep sides of the wall. Mounds B and C contained a series of very large post holes 2'-3' in diameter. These mounds appear to have been built as a single, continuous event. Mound D is a significantly large and complex burial mound 20' high and more than 100' in diameter. Mound E, also a burial mound and the first of the Kolomoki mounds to have been excavated scientifically, lies partly exposed within the Kolomoki Museum. The west half of Mound E abuts the west end of the museum. Mounds F and G were "ceremonial" mounds about 60' long, 50' wide, and 6' high.

DIRECTIONS: From Early County Courthouse in Blakely, follow U. S. Route 27 N 2.1 mi. to Kolomoki Rd., then go N on Kolomoki Rd. 4.5 mi. to Kolomoki Mounds State Park, on E. From the courthouse in Cuthbert follow U. S. Route 27 S approximately 20 mi. to Bluffton, go S on Kolomoki Rd. 4.5 mi. to Kolomoki Mounds State Park, on W. Signs provide directions to the park (Figure 55).

PUBLIC USE: Season and hours: Grounds are open 7:00 AM-10:00 PM, daily. **Fees:** None. **Recreational facilities:** Picnic areas, restrooms, trails, camping, swimming, boating, fishing. **Restrictions:** Georgia State Law prohibits digging for or collecting artifacts on state owned land.

EDUCATIONAL FACILITIES: Museum: A museum describing and interpreting the cultural history of Kolomoki is located near the west entrance to the park. A dominant exhibit is the exposed view of the partially excavated burial Mound E which shows skeletons and grave goods in place. Other exhibits focus on the basic economy of the Kolomoki people, house and mound construction, artisan activities, and pottery. **Museum hours:** 9:00 AM-5:00 PM, Tuesday through Saturday; 2:00-5:30 PM, Sunday. Closed Mondays (except Memorial Day and Labor Day), Thanksgiving, and Christmas. **Fees:** Admission is $1.50 adults (13 years and above), $.75 children (6-12 years); children (5 years and under) are admitted free. Group rates are available. **Bookstore:** A modest selection of books is available for sale at the museum.

FOR ADDITIONAL INFORMATION: Contact: Superintendent, Kolomoki Mounds State Park, Route 1, Blakely, GA 31723, 912-723-5296. **Read:** Sears, William H. 1956. Excavations at Kolomoki, Final Report. University of Georgia Series in Anthropology, no. 5.

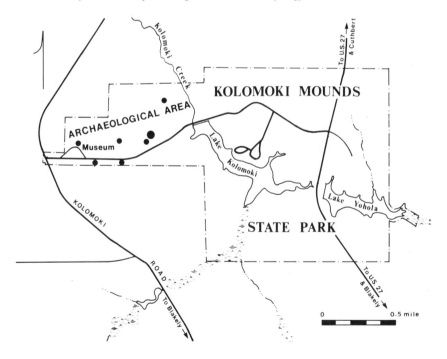

Figure 55. Location of Kolomoki Ceremonial Center.

21. Sapelo Shell Ring

Late Archaic Shell Ring
McIntosh County, Georgia

Near High Point, at the northwest corner of Sapelo Island, one of the largest sea islands of Georgia, was a major concentration of aboriginal shell features. Three shell rings were reported here in 1872 by William McKinley, the first person to provide a technical description of the site. McKinley described mound-circle 1 as being 240' wide, between 9' and 20' high, and 30' across the base of the wall. Circles 2 and 3 were 210' and 150' wide, respectively; both were about 3' high, and 20' across the base, and were in "an open field long cultivated." Clarence B. Moore described circle 1, in 1897, as being greater than 300' across, 5'-7' high, and about 50' across the base. Surrounding these circles were hundreds of shell-mounds about 3' high and 20'-50' across the base, scattered randomly over an area of 100 acres or more. At least one burial mound was located on the west side of the island, about 3 miles south of the shell features.

Today, only the largest of the three shell rings — which is also the largest shell ring known — is apparent (Figure 11). The large shell ring has been disturbed, the most conspicuous damage being a relatively recent excavation scar through the west wall of the ring. The ring is located adjacent to Mud River in an open forest of old-growth oak and cedar. The other features in the High Point area have been destroyed or altered by years of cultivation and by mining the shells for road fill and tabby construction. (The remains of several old buildings constructed, in part, of tabby can still be seen on Sapelo Island.) The burial mound is still intact.

The shell in the surviving ring consists largely of oysters, with some conch, clam and mussel shell also present. The ring has been radiocarbon dated to about 4,100-3,800 years ago, placing it in the Late Archaic Period. Also found within the Sapelo ring were fragments of fiber-tempered ceramic pottery, some of the oldest ceramic pottery known from North America. Much of the debris found in the walls (ash lenses, fireplaces, midden pits, etc.) indicates that dwellings were located either near or directly on the ring.

The Sapelo Island shell ring is impressive and well worth a visit by any person interested in seeing fine examples of remaining aboriginal mound-like structures. Access to the ring, however, is restricted. The Georgia Department of Natural Resources offers tours of Sapelo Island two (winter) or three (summer) times each week, but *the shell ring is included only on the long tour which is offered only on the last Wednesday of each month.* Reservations for participation in the tours are made through the McIntosh County Chamber of Commerce; tickets must be picked up at the Chamber's Welcome Center in Darien one-half hour before the tour departs from Meridian, which is located about 9 miles northeast of the Welcome Center.

DIRECTIONS: The McIntosh County Chamber of Commerce Welcome Center is located on the E side of U. S. Route 17, N of the bridge over the Darien River, in Darien. From the Welcome Center, go 0.1 mi. N on U. S. Route 17 to Georgia State Route 14, then NE on Georgia Route 14 for 8 mi. to Sapelo Island Dock sign in Meridian, then E at sign 0.9 mi. to dock. Notice that specific areas at the dock are designated for visitors' parking (Figure 56).

PUBLIC USE: Season and hours: Summer tour schedule (June through August) — Wednesday and Friday, 8:30 AM-12:30 PM; Saturday, 9:00 AM-1:00 PM; Winter tour schedule (September through May), Wednesday, 8:30 AM-12:30 PM; Saturday, 9:00 AM-1:00 PM. Last Wednesday of each month, long walking tour, 8:30 AM-5:00 PM. **Reservations:** Reservations, required for assured participation, can be made by telephone with McIntosh County Chamber of Commerce, 912-437-6684. **Fees:** All tours, $5.00 per person. **Food service:** None. *Visitors taking the long tour should bring a sack lunch.* **Transportation:** Boat and bus transportation is provided from and back to the Sapelo Island Dock, and on the island.

EDUCATIONAL FACILITIES: Tour guide: All tours are guided by Ms. Cornelia Bailey, a lifelong resident of Sapelo Island. Ms. Bailey provides a comprehensive, intimate introduction to the Island and is a highlight of the tour. **Special group activities:** Group and class tours may be arranged through the Georgia Department of Natural Resources, Sapelo Island, GA 31327, 912-485-2251.

FOR ADDITIONAL INFORMATION: Contact: McIntosh County Chamber of Commerce, P. O. Box 1497, Darien, GA 31305, 912-437-6684 *or* Historic Sites Division, Department of Natural Resources, 270 Washington Street SW, Atlanta, GA 30334, 404-656-3530. **Read:** (1) Waring, Antonio J., Jr., and Lewis H. Larson, Jr. 1977. The shell ring on Sapelo Island. Pp. 263-278 in Stephen Williams (ed.), The Waring Papers: The Collected Works of Antonio J. Waring, Jr. Papers of the Peabody Museum of Archaeology and Ethnology, Harvard University, vol. 58 (Revised edition). (2) Simpkins, Daniel L. 1980. A preliminary report on test excavations at the Sapelo Island Shell Ring. Pp. 61-75 in Daniel P. Juengst, (ed.), Sapelo Papers: Researches in the History and Prehistory of Sapelo Island, Georgia. West Georgia College Studies in the Social Sciences, vol. 19.

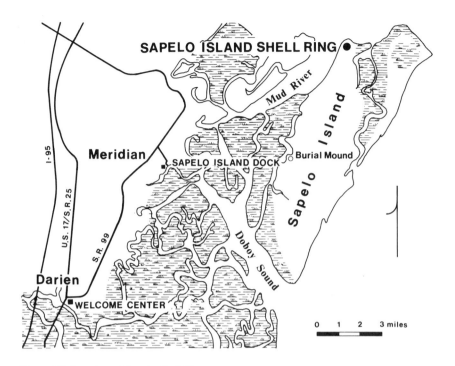

Figure 56. Location of Sapelo Shell Ring.

22. Canaveral Seashore Middens

Late Archaic and Woodland Shell Middens
Volusia County, Florida

Two large publicly accessible shell middens are located in the northern part of Canaveral National Seashore, a unit of the National Park Service. The larger, less disturbed, and better known of these middens is Turtle Mound; the other is Castle Windy Midden. Both are located along the west edge of the barrier island, overlooking the northern traces of Mosquito Lagoon, and both are composed primarily of oyster shell with lesser quantities of shells of other mollusks. These middens are attributed to people of the late St. Johns culture and the historic Timucuan Indians, and are considered to have been built between A.D. 800-1400 primarily with shell and other debris produced by the winter exploitation of the coastal resources. The Indians who built these middens, and the large Green Mound a short distance to the north, probably spent their summers inland along the St. Johns River exploiting resources of that region.

Turtle Mound — which has also been called Mt. Velvidere, The Rock, and Mount Tucker — is about 30' high in the center; each end is approximately 5' higher. From Mosquito Lagoon, this midden can be seen to stand well above the surrounding land surface. The mound is reached by a short trail — actually a boardwalk with rails — leading from the parking lot to each of the twin peaks of the midden. Interpretive signs are located at several places along the boardwalk and comment upon several aspects of Timucuan life style, social organization, and ecology. Panoramic views of the Atlantic Ocean, Merritt Island, Mosquito Lagoon, and the mainland beyond are available from the top of the two crests of Turtle Mound, and allow the visitor to relate to the suggestion that the Timucuan Indians might also have used this midden as a lookout facility. Turtle Mound is densely vegetated with, in some places, an impenetrable coastal scrub forest, and it is consequently not possible to obtain a clear visual impression of its size and shape, at least from a land vantage point.

Castle Windy Midden is approximately 20' high, although it has been partially destroyed by erosion and the mining of its shells for road construction. This midden lies about 0.5 mile west of the park road and is reached by a nature trail that is about 1 mile long, round trip. Unlike the boardwalk at Turtle Mound, this trail is on natural surface; it leads tunnel-like, away from the Castle Windy parking area, into the wind-salt-and-sand sculpted coastal scrub forest. This trail crosses some low shell middens and identifies, at one numbered station, yaupon — the holly used by many southeastern Indians to make their *Black Drink.* The trail ends at the edge of Mosquito Lagoon, after passing alongside a cut through the south end of Castle Windy Midden. Perhaps the best view of this midden is from along the nature trail after numbered station 13; from here, through the relatively open forest, the configuration of this feature can be seen clearly.

DIRECTIONS: Exit Interstate 95 onto Florida State Route 44, go E 3 mi. into New Smyrna Beach, take Florida State Route A1A E, then S, 11 mi. to Turtle Mound (0.7 mi. S of entrance to Canaveral National Seashore) on W. Continue S another 3.5 mi. to Castle Windy parking area on E. Castle Windy Midden is ca. 0.5 mi. W, by nature trail (1.0 mi., round trip) (Figure 57).

PUBLIC USE: Season and hours: The National Seashore grounds are open 6:00 AM-6:00 PM daily when on Standard Time; 6:00 AM-8:00 PM daily when on Daylight Savings Time. **Fees:** $3.00 per vehicle per day; $10.00 per year. **Recreational facilities:** Picnic areas, restrooms, swimming, trails, primitive camping (reservations required). **Restrictions:** Climbing on or otherwise disturbing the middens is prohibited.

EDUCATIONAL FACILITIES: Visitor center: Some exhibits on the natural history of Canaveral National Seashore are housed in the Eldora Visitor Center, but information about the middens is not included. **Visitor center hours:** 8:00 AM- 4:30 PM Monday-Friday, 8:30 AM-4:00 PM, Saturday-Sunday. **Fees:** Admission to grounds includes access to visitor center. **Trails:** Interpretive trails are located at Castle Windy Midden and Turtle Mound. Signs placed along the boardwalk interpret the Turtle Mound Trail. The Castle Windy Trail Guide interprets numbered stations along the Castle Windy Trail; the guide is available at the visitor center or in the box at the trailhead.

FOR ADDITIONAL INFORMATION: Contact: Superintendent, Canaveral National Seashore, P. O. Box 6447, Titusville, FL 32782, 305-267-1110. **Read:** Bullen, Ripley P., and Frederick W. Sleight. 1959. Archaeological Investigations at the Castle Windy Midden, Florida. The William Bryant Foundation, American Studies Report 1.

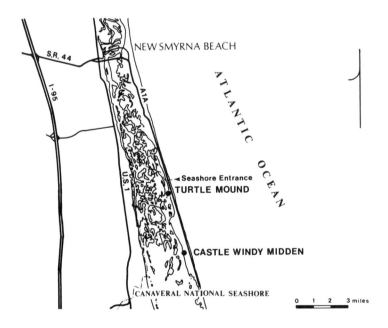

Figure 57. Location of Turtle Mound and Castle Windy Midden.

23. Mount Royal

Late Woodland Burial Mound
Putnam County, Florida

"At about fifty yards distance from the landing place, stands a magnificent Indian mount... But what greatly contributed towards completing the magnificence of the scene, was a noble Indian highway, which led from the great mount, on a straight line, three quarters of a mile, first through a point or wing of the orange grove, and continuing thence through an awful forest of live oaks, it was terminated by palms and laurel magnolias, on the verge of an oblong artificial lake, which was on the edge of an extensive green level savanna. This grand highway was about fifty yards wide, sunk a little below the common level, and the earth thrown up on each side, making a bank of about two feet high. Neither nature nor art could any where present a more striking contrast, as you approached this savanna." (Bartram, 1791, pp. 101-2)

The Mount Royal site includes a burial mound, scattered small shell middens, an artificial pond, and a sunken road connecting the mound and pond (Figure 24C). The mound was about 16' high and 555' in circumference when it was investigated by Clarence Moore in 1893-94; other reports describe it as being somewhat larger. The mound was built of sand obtained from a borrow pit about 3/4 of a mile away. The removal of this sand created an artificial lake. The borrow pit and lake and the mound were connected by a sunken causeway that was about 2,600' long and 150' wide. Parallel ridges about 2'-3' high and 10' wide were located along either side of the causeway. The mound was built between A.D. 1200-1500 by Indians of the Late St. Johns culture.

Mount Royal was excavated by Moore, who determined that the mound had been built in stages for the burial of prominent leaders. The site is important archeologically because it produced large quantities of grave goods unusual for the St. Johns River region. This material provided evidence of long distance trade with Mississippian people during Late St. Johns time. The sunken road, similar to those found in sites in the Lake Okeechobee Basin, suggests interaction with that region too.

Recently, this site has been acquired by the State of Florida and restored; it is now managed as a publicly accessible archeological site. The mound is fenced, but a gate allows foot traffic to the mound. The feature is generally grass covered, mown, and supports some large trees which give the site a park-like appearance. An interpretive sign is located in the shelter near the mound. The protection, restoration and management of this site is an excellent example of cooperation among a private landowner, the State and professional and amateur archeologists.

DIRECTIONS: From U. S. Route 17, northbound, take Florida Route 308 W 8.5 mi. from N side of Crescent City, then go N on Florida State Route 309 1.3 mi. to Ft. Gates Ferry Road (unpaved), then go S on Ft. Gates Ferry Rd. 0.25 mi., then continue S on Mt. Royal Ave. (paved) 0.4 mi. to Indian Mound Rd. (unpaved), then go SW on Indian Mound Rd. 0.15 mi. to Mount Royal. From U. S. Route 17, southbound, exit onto Florida State Route 309 at Satsuma and go about 8 mi. S to Ft. Gates Ferry Rd., then continue as above (Figure 58).

PUBLIC USE: Season and hours: The grounds are accessible 24 hours each day. **Fees:** None.

FOR ADDITIONAL INFORMATION: Contact: Bureau of Archaeological Research, Division of Historical Resources, Florida Department of State, Tallahassee, FL 32399-0250, 904-487-2299. **Read:** Moore, Clarence B. 1894-96. Certain sand mounds of the St. Johns River, Florida. Journal of the Academy of Natural Sciences of Philadelphia, vol. 10, nos. 1 and 2.

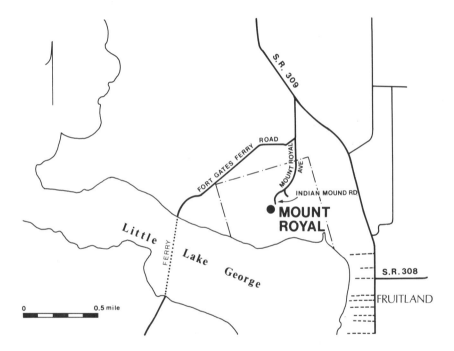

Figure 58. Location of Mount Royal.

106

24. Alexander Springs Midden

Late Archaic Shell Midden
Lake County, Florida

Jeffries Wyman, curator of the Peabody Museum at Harvard University, made several trips to Florida where he studied the freshwater shell heaps and other archeological features of the St. Johns River region. During the winter of 1873, Wyman visited Alexander Springs, from where he wrote to his son on February 16: "Our camp is on the slope of a sand hill and is nice and dry and as good as any place we have been in. . .The water is as blue and clear as possible. The fish swimming about, and the shells at the bottom can be seen with the greatest distinctness. . ." (George Gifford, Dear Jeffie. . ., p. 57). Two and one-half years later, in a posthumously published monograph titled *Fresh-Water Shell Mounds of the St. John's River, Florida,* Wyman stated "The largest numbers of shells which we saw were in the Wekiva River, Juniper Creek, Alexander's Spring Creek, and in the lagoon above, and in the large bay below, Bartram's Mound. The bottom in all of these, wherever left exposed by the aquatic plants, was seen to be covered with them. . ." (p. 12).

Indians that inhabited the St. Johns River region long before Wyman's visit also found the waters of the area bountiful and left numerous — sometimes very large — shell heaps along the river and tributary creeks as testimony to this fact. One of the few remaining publicly accessible middens resulting from the use of this resource is located in the picnic area at the Alexander Springs Campground, Ocala National Forest. Here, on the side of a gently sloping hill a few feet above Alexander Springs Creek, is a low, unspectacular midden composed largely of small snail shells. This feature is located beneath the two cement picnic tables and nearby trees which are nearest the canoe livery. The midden is covered with a thin layer of sand which provides some protection against pedestrian traffic. As a result of the sand, the shell surface cannot be seen by visitors but the location, shape and size of the gently rounded feature are visible.

DIRECTIONS: Northbound on Florida State Route 19, about 5 mi. N of Altoona, go E on Lake County Road 445 5.2 mi. to Alexander Springs Campground on N side of road. Eastbound or westbound on Florida State Route 40, at Astor Park, go S on Lake County Road 445A 0.5 mi., then S on Lake County Road 445 6.1 mi. to Alexander Springs Campground. The picnic area is 0.2 mi. into the campground (Figure 59).

PUBLIC USE: Season and hours: Alexander Springs Campground is open 8:00 AM-8:00 PM daily. **Fees:** A user fee of $1.05 is charged. **Recreational facilities:** Picnic area, restrooms, canoeing, swimming, snorkeling, scuba diving, camping, foot trail. **Restrictions:** Animals other than seeing-eye dogs are not permitted in the picnic or swimming areas. Dogs in other areas must be on a leash no more than 6' in length. Disturbing or removing archeological resources is strictly prohibited. Additional regulations are posted in the Campground.

EDUCATIONAL FACILITIES: Trails: The self guiding Timucuan Indian Trail (0.8 mi. round trip) leads through the local subtropical vegetation and interprets the use of native plant resources by Indians. **Staff programs:** Evening interpretive programs are provided during summer months.

FOR ADDITIONAL INFORMATION: Contact: Alexander Springs Recreation Area *or* Seminole District Office, U. S. Forest Service, Florida Highway 19 North, Eustis, FL 32726, 904-669-3522 (Alexander Springs Recreation Area) or 904-357-3721 (Seminole District Office).

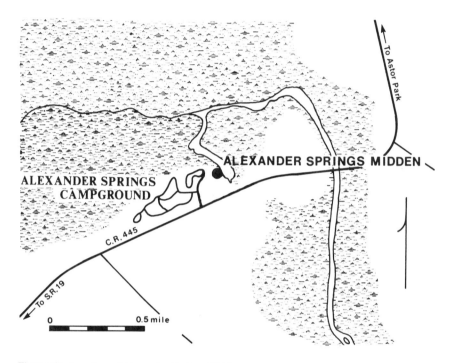

Figure 59. Location of Alexander Springs Midden.

25. Hontoon Island Mound

Late Archaic and Woodland Shell Midden
Volusia County, Florida

A large shell midden, nearly 30' high and 200' long, is located on the west side of Hontoon Island in Hontoon Island State Park. Like other fresh water shell mounds along the St. Johns River, this one is composed largely of snail shells. "Any one who for the first time views the larger ones," wrote Jeffries Wyman (1875, p. 11), "might well be excused for doubting that such immense quantities of small shells could have been brought together by human labor, aided only by such appliances as the builders of these mounds may be supposed to have possessed."

This midden lies at the end of the park's 1.2 mile nature trail. (The 2.4 mile round trip walk on this trail requires about 1.5 hours for the average visitor to complete.) This midden has not been excavated by professional archeologists, but investigations are pending as this book goes to press. Typically, fresh water shell middens along the St. Johns River began to accumulate during the late Archaic Period and continued to be enlarged periodically during the Woodland Period.

Many other shell mounds were located on or near Hontoon Island in the past, including two — one on either side of the St. Johns River — where the parking lot and park headquarters are now located. According to Wyman (1875, pp. 27-29), "That on the left bank, on Hontoon Island, is of gigantic size, covers several acres, and consists of two ridges both parallel to the river. . .The mound on the right bank is smaller, not over six feet high and consists of a low ridge running parallel with the river and of about the same length as that on the opposite side." Detached, smaller burial mounds occurred near these large middens.

DIRECTIONS: From Florida State Route 44 W of De Land, go S on Old New York Ave. 1.5 mi. to Hontoon Rd., then S on Hontoon Rd. 2.5 mi., then E and S on River Ridge Rd. 0.9 mi. to Hontoon Island State Park parking area. Free passenger ferry service, operated by the State, provides access to Hontoon Island from the parking lot (Figure 60).

PUBLIC USE: Season and hours: Grounds are open 8:00 AM-Sunset, daily. Ferry service operates 9:00 AM-1 hour before sunset, daily. Private watercraft may use the State Park docks during daylight hours with no charge. **Fees:** None for day use. Fees are charged for primitive tent camping ($6.42 per night), cabins ($12.84 per night), or overnight use of boat docks ($6.42 and $8.52 per night). **Recreational facilities:** Picnic area, restrooms, nature trail, primitive tent camping, cabins (reservations required), boat landing, fishing. **Restrictions:** Archeological, floral, and faunal resources may not be disturbed or removed from the park. Pets must be on 6' hand held leash, and are not permitted in camping area. Intoxicants are not permitted in the park.

FOR ADDITIONAL INFORMATION: Contact: Ranger in Charge, Hontoon Island State Park, 2309 River Ridge Rd., De Land, FL 32720, 904-734-7158. **Read:** Wyman, Jeffries. 1875. Fresh-Water Shell Mounds of the St. John's River, Florida. Memoirs of the Peabody Academy of Science, Fourth Memoir.

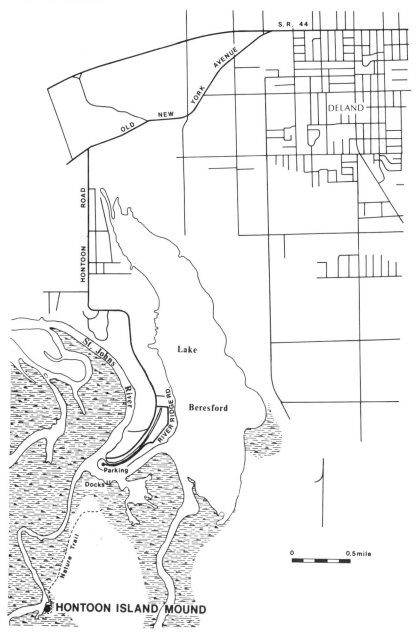

Figure 60. Location of Hontoon Island Midden.

26. Jupiter Inlet Lighthouse Midden

Woodland Shell Midden
Palm Beach County, Florida

This midden is located on the north side of the Loxahatchee River, immediately west of the Intracoastal Waterway, on the Jupiter Inlet U. S. Coast Guard Station. A lighthouse has been built on the midden. The Loxahatchee Historical Society maintains a small museum in a building adjacent to the lighthouse. This museum contains an exhibit of artifacts from the Jupiter Inlet Midden I located across the Loxahatchee River (Jupiter Inlet) from the lighthouse.

DIRECTIONS: Exit U. S. Route 1, about 0.4 mi. N of bridge over Loxahatchee River (Jupiter Inlet), onto Florida State Route 707, go E on Route 707 0.05 mi. to Captain Armour's Way, then go S on Captain Armour's Way 0.6 mi. to lighthouse (Figure 61).

PUBLIC USE: Season and hours: 12:00 noon-2:30 PM, Sunday. Closed holidays.

EDUCATIONAL FACILITIES: Museum: The Loxahatchee Historical Society maintains a small museum in a building adjacent to the lighthouse. **Museum hours:** Same as grounds hours (above). **Fees:** Contributions are accepted. **Bookstore:** A modest selection of educational publications is available.

FOR ADDITIONAL INFORMATION: Contact: Loxahatchee Historical Society, P. O. Box 1506, Jupiter, FL 33458, 305-747-6639.

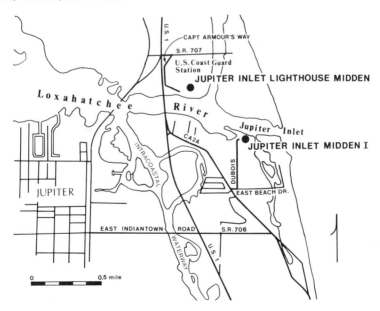

Figure 61. Location of Jupiter Inlet Lighthouse Midden and Jupiter Inlet Midden I.

27. Jupiter Inlet Midden

Woodland Shell Midden
Palm Beach County, Florida

When Jonathan Dickinson's party of travelers bound from Jamaica to Philadelphia was shipwrecked off central Florida in 1696, they were captured by Indians and taken to the nearby village of Hobe ("hoe-bay"). After a brief period of detention, they were released and sent on their way, on foot, northward. Historians have identified Hobe as the village of the Jeaga Indians that was located on the south side of Jupiter Inlet, Palm Beach County. Also at this village was one of the notably large clam and oyster shell middens of the Florida Atlantic Coast, a feature now known as the Jupiter Inlet I, or DuBois, Midden. In 1897, Harry DuBois built a house on top of this midden; the structure, with additions, is still standing. The house has been restored and furnished by the Loxahatchee Historical Society and — with the midden — forms the historical centerpiece of DuBois Park, a Palm Beach County facility.

The age of this midden is not known for certain. Artifacts collected from the midden and the surrounding area indicate that Indians were using the site as early as 3,000 years ago. In 1963, William Sears excavated part of the site. Sears' investigations reached to a depth of 51" and documented use of the midden between about A.D. 750-1750. He believed that further excavations would show that the site was used from about 500 B.C.

When Dickinson's party was at Hobe, the midden probably measured about 600' in length and 20' in height. The midden is now much smaller. During the first half of the 20th Century, substantial quantities of shell were removed for use in road construction. One significant sale was made in 1917 when the town of Lake Park obtained a large amount of the shell mound for road building material. Today, the midden varies from 5'-15' in height, 97'-165' in width, and 180'-345' in length. Many other middens occur in this area.

DIRECTIONS: From U. S. Route 1, southbound, exit onto Palm Beach County Road CA2A 0.2 mi. S of bridge over Loxahatchee River, go 0.8 mi. S on CA2A to East Beach Dr., then E ca. 200 feet on East Beach Dr. to DuBois Rd., then N 0.3 mi. to DuBois Park. Northbound on U. S. 1, go E on Florida State Route 706 (East Indiantown Rd.) 0.5 mi. to CA2A, then N on CA2A 0.4 mi. to East Beach Dr., then continue as above (Figure 61).

PUBLIC USE: Season and hours: Grounds are open daily 1 hour before sunrise to 1 hour after sunset. **Fees:** None. **Recreational facilities:** Picnic areas, restrooms, fishing, boating, trails. **Restrictions:** Dogs are not permitted in the park.

EDUCATIONAL FACILITIES: Museum: The Loxahatchee Historical Society has furnished the DuBois House with early 19th Century period pieces and operates this house as a museum. **Museum hours:** 1:00-3:30 PM, Sunday. Closed holidays. **Fees:** Contributions are accepted. **Bookstore:** A modest selection of educational publications is available.

FOR ADDITIONAL INFORMATION: Contact: Loxahatchee Historical Society, P. O. Box 1506, Jupiter, FL 33458, 305-747-6639.

28. Arch Creek Midden

Late Woodland Shell Midden
North Miami Beach, Dade County, Florida

Arch Creek Midden is located in Arch Creek Park, an 8 acre tract of land owned by the State of Florida and managed by the Dade County Parks and Recreation Department. This feature originally encompassed about 5 acres, but much of it has been disturbed by urban development. This midden is formed largely of shells of conch and oyster that were harvested by Tequesta and related Indians living in the area between 500 B.C. and A.D. 1300. A single burial has been found in this feature. Materials from the midden are on display in the small park museum.

Arch Creek Park preserves an island of oak hammock (upland hardwood) vegetation and associated prehistoric and historic sites within the northern Miami suburban area. This park also preserves the site of the natural limestone arch from which the local place names derive and the site of a 19th Century Coontie mill. (Coontie is the Seminole name for a cycad, *Zamia pumila,* from which starch was obtained. During the historic period, pioneers also used this cycad as a source of starch.) Arch Creek is a pleasant spot at which to stop, rest, and discover a little about the natural and cultural history of the Miami area.

DIRECTIONS: From U. S. Route 1 (Biscayne Blvd.) in North Miami, go W on Florida State Route 916 (NE 135th St.) for 0.15 mi. to Arch Creek Park on N. From Interstate Route 95, go E on 135th St. 2.9 mi. to park (Figure 62).

PUBLIC USE: Season and hours: 9:00 AM-5:00 PM daily. Closed Thanksgiving, Christmas, New Years. **Fees:** None. **Recreational facilities:** Picnic area, restrooms, trail. **Restrictions:** Dogs, alcohol, and open fires are prohibited. Removal of artifacts or natural objects from the park is prohibited.

EDUCATIONAL FACILITIES: Museum: The small park museum has on display objects representing the last Ice Age of Florida and the natural history, prehistory, and history of the Arch Creek area. **Museum hours:** Same as grounds hours (above). **Fees:** None. **Trails:** The Tequesta Nature Trail extends through most of the park. An interpretive guidebook, keyed to numbered stations, is available. **Staff programs:** Each Saturday, at 1:00 PM, a staff-guided tour of the park is offered at no charge. **Special group activities:** Staff-directed programs for groups are available with prior arrangement; these include trail walks, nature workshops, slide shows, and archeological "digs" (all artifacts found, however, must be left at the museum).

FOR ADDITIONAL INFORMATION: Contact: Manager, Arch Creek Park, 1855 NE 135th St., North Miami, FL 33161, 305-944-6111 *or* Archeologist, Historic Preservation Division, Office of County Manager, 111 SW 5th Ave., Suite 101, Miami, FL 33130, 305-545-4228. **Read:** (1) Laxson, Dan D. 1957. The Arch Creek Site. Florida Anthropologist, vol. 10 (nos. 3-4), pp. 1-13. (2) Broward County Archaeological Society and Miami-West India Archaeological Society. 1975. The Arch Creek Site, Dade County. Florida Anthropologist, vol. 28, pp. 1-13.

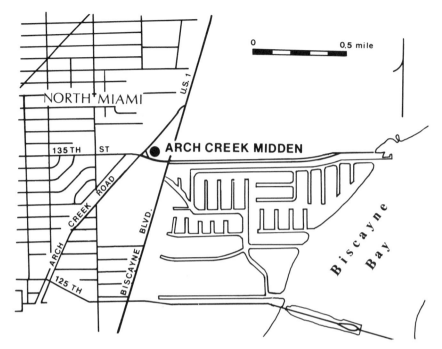

Figure 62. Location of Arch Creek Midden.

29. Cutler Burial Mound

Late Woodland Burial Mound
Perrine, Dade County, Florida

A short distance inland from the southeast corner of Florida lies the Atlantic Coastal Ridge, a slightly elevated surface that trends generally north-south. Streams flowing eastward from the Everglades descended through this ridge toward nearby Biscayne Bay and the Atlantic Ocean. Hardwood hammocks (upland forest communities) developed on this ridge, while mangrove forests grew toward the coast. Typically, late Woodland Indians of the Glades culture — including the historic Tequesta Indians — located their villages on this Ridge. One such village was on land that is now a part of the Charles Deering Estate, a public park overlooking Biscayne Bay that is maintained by the Dade County Park and Recreation Department.

Near, and probably associated with, the Indian village on the Deering Estate is a low, conical burial mound. This feature — the Cutler Burial Mound — is about 6.5' high and 75' in circumference and is made of sand. The mound has not been excavated by professional archeologists, and its age is not known for certain — although it is similar to late Woodland mounds in the area that date about A.D. 1000-1500. An excavation of the mound in 1876 by Henry E. Perrine, an amateur investigator, located several skeletons. Perrine's description of the burials is one of the few available on the mortuary practices of the south Florida Indians. Almost all of the skulls had been buried with the face turned down and the tops toward the center of the mound. The heads apparently had been separated from the rest of the skeleton before interment.

The Deering Estate preserves the 358 acre estate and winter residence of Charles Deering, chairman of the board of International Harvester from 1904-1918. Upon the grounds are located some of the largest remnants of native plant communities in Dade County, along with a rich variety of other paleontological, archeological and historical resources.

DIRECTIONS: From U. S. Route 1 in Perrine, exit E onto 168th St. (Richmond Dr.) and go 2.2 mi. to SW 72nd Ave., then N 0.05 mi. on SW 72nd Ave. to entrance to Deering Park on E (Figure 63).

PUBLIC USE: Season and hours: 9:00 AM-5:00 PM, Saturday and Sunday. Open some holidays. **Fees:** Adults (13 years and above) $4.00, children (6-12 years) $2.00, children less than 6 years free. **Recreational facilities:** Picnic areas, restrooms. **Restrictions:** Access to the hammock and the Cutler Mound is by guided tour only. Pets are not permitted on the estate grounds.

EDUCATIONAL FACILITIES: Staff programs: Guided tours of the grounds are provided daily. Guided canoe trips are also offered. A Nature Day Camp is offered during summer months, and interpretive programs are offered at other times during the year. Contact estate for specific dates.

FOR ADDITIONAL INFORMATION: Contact: Manager, The Charles Deering Estate, 16701 SW 72nd Ave., Miami, FL 33157, 305-235-1668 *or* Archeologist, Historic Preservation Division, Office of County Manager, 111 SW 5th Ave., Suite 101, Miami, FL 33130, 305-545-4228.

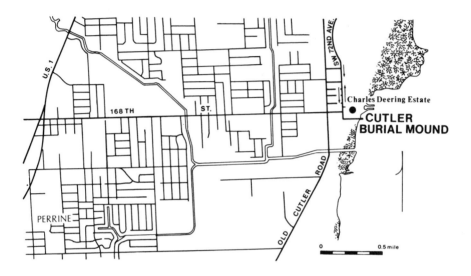

Figure 63. Location of Cutler Burial Mound.

30. Mound Key

Late Woodland Key Dweller Site
Lee County, Florida

Mound Key was one of the largest and most elaborate occupation sites of the Calusa Indians of southwest Florida. This largely artificial island is some 70-80 acres in area, and contains several mounds, artificial terraces, and debris middens. Among the mounds are one small burial mound, two large oval-shaped mounds probably used as dwelling sites, and a large platform mound that is presently about 31' high and 200' square at the base. Beneath the platform mound and the larger oval mound is an extensive terrace that varies from 5'-15' in height. A canal passes between the platform and large oval mound. Mound Key is representative of the Calusa key dweller sites that were concentrated on Florida's southwest coast between Charlotte Harbor and Marco Island.

The Calusa settlement at Mound Key has been identified as the town of Calos. Here, in 1566, Pedro Menendez, recently appointed governor of Spanish Florida, made contact with the Calusa and their powerful king, Calos.

Mound Key is a detached unit of Koreshan State Historic Site lying about 0.4 miles southwest of the mouth of the Estero River in Estero Bay. Access to this island is by water, the most generally convenient route being via the Estero River from either Koreshan State Historic Site boat landing (a distance of four miles) or nearby private landings or boat rentals. The State Historic Site does not provide transportation to the island, and boats cannot be rented at the State Site. The island is in a primitive condition, so visitors should not expect facilities or interpretation. No drinking water is available on the island. Also, visitors unfamiliar with navigating small boats through mangrove swamps should take adequate precautions that they not become disoriented during the journey.

Koreshan State Historic Site preserves the site and structures where was undertaken, beginning in the 1890s, a pioneer attempt to create a new religion, Koreshan Universeology. The founder of this movement, Cyrus Teed of Chicago, died in 1908 and the Koreshan movement subsequently lost momentum — although the Koreshan Unity still continues.

DIRECTIONS: From U. S. Route 41, 0.4 mi. S of Estero, go W on Corkscrew Rd. 0.2 mi. to Koreshan State Historic Site entrance. The boat ramp, with adjacent parking, is about 0.5 mi. into the park (Figure 64).

PUBLIC USE: Season and hours: The grounds of Koreshan State Historic Site — including Mound Key — are open 8:00 AM-Sunset, daily. **Fees:** Admission $1.00 for vehicle operator, $.50 for each additional passenger; children under 6 years of age admitted free. **Recreational facilities:** Picnic area, restrooms, camping, nature trail, boat landing. **Staff programs:** Park rangers conduct tours of the Koreshan settlement site daily. Campfire programs and guided walks are offered according to seasonal demand. **Restrictions:** Camping on Mound Key is prohibited. State law prohibits the disturbance or removal of archeological sites and resources, plant life and animal life. Intoxicants are not permitted in the park. Pets must be on a 6' hand held leash and well behaved at all times. Pets are not allowed in the camping area or Koreshan settlement site.

FOR ADDITIONAL INFORMATION: Contact: Park Manager, Koreshan State Historic Site, P. O. Box 7, Estero, FL 33928, 813-992-0311. **Read:** Schell, Rolfe F. 1962. 1,000 Years on Mound Key. Fort Myers Beach: The Island Press.

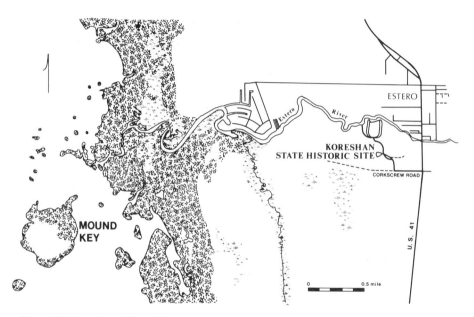

Figure 64. Location of Mound Key.

31. Sarasota County Mound

Woodland Shell Midden
Sarasota County, Florida

Sarasota County Mound is a relatively large shell midden, composed of a variety of shells of marine shellfish, located near the end of Paulson Point along the shore of Lemon Bay. This midden originally measured some 750' in length, 300' in width, and 13' in depth at its maximum dimensions. The midden began to accumulate at the beginning of the Woodland Period, about 3,000 years ago, as human populations moved into south Florida. The midden was used until the beginning of the Safety Harbor phase about A.D. 1350. Water level has risen perhaps as much as 4'-5' in this area since the midden began to accumulate, so much of the feature is now below water level. Other parts of the feature have been separated from the main part of the midden by the construction of mosquito control and boat canals. One interesting aspect of the archeology of this site is that an unusually high frequency of projectile points found during test excavations in 1965 and 1966 were made of quartz. Quartz artifacts are rare in Florida, especially south Florida.

The Sarasota County Mound is now the centerpiece of Indian Mound Park, a Sarasota County facility located in Englewood. The higher part of the original midden is now within the park; it is irregularly shaped and is about 8' high. The feature is densely vegetated, but several paths lead across the mound and it is easily recognized as a large shell midden.

DIRECTIONS: From Florida State Route 775 in Englewood, 0.4 mi. N of Lemon Bay Cemetery and 0.9 mi. N of the Sarasota County/Charlotte County boundary, go W on Cowles St. 0.5 mi., then N on Magnolia St. 0.05 mi., then W on Fray St. 0.05 mi., then S on Winson St. 0.1 mi. to Indian Mound Park. The midden is in the grove of trees ahead, beyond the parking lot (Figure 65).

PUBLIC USE: Season and hours: The grounds are open to pedestrians 24 hours each day and to vehicles 6:00 AM-Midnight, daily. **Fees:** None. **Recreation facilities:** Picnic area, restrooms, boat landing, fishing. **Restrictions:** Pets, open fires, and glass beverage containers are prohibited in the park.

FOR ADDITIONAL INFORMATION: Contact: Sarasota County Parks and Recreation Department, 5531 Pinkney Ave., Sarasota, FL 34233, 813-951-5572. **Read:** Bullen, Ripley P. 1971. The Sarasota County Mound, Englewood, Florida. Florida Anthropologist, vol. 24, no. 1, pp. 1-30.

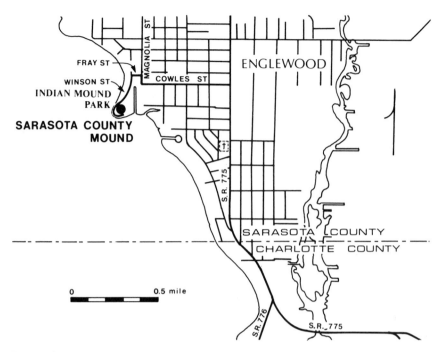

Figure 65. Location of Sarasota County Mound.

32. Madira Bickel Mounds

Late Woodland and Mississippian Mound Complex
Terra Ceia Island, Manatee County, Florida

The Madira Bickel Mounds are parts of the Terra Ceia Site, occupied from perhaps 500 B.C. to about A.D. 1600. The site included two burial mounds, an extensive shell midden, and a platform mound. The platform mound and one burial mound are included in the 10 acre Madira Bickel Mounds State Archaeological Site, the first tract in Florida to be designated a State Archaeological Site. A short trail leads from the parking area to the top of the platform mound.

The low burial mound is the older feature. This mound was started during Weeden Island time (about A.D. 700-1000) and continued in use through the Safety Harbor period (A.D. 1300-1600 or beyond). Much of this sand mound, and the burials in it, was destroyed when it was used for road building material. However, when Ripley Bullen excavated part of this mound in 1950 he located evidence of more than 30 burials. Today this mound is about 18" high and 100' in diameter.

The platform mound, called the Madira Bickel, or Bickel Ceremonial, Mound, was built of shell and sand during Safety Harbor time. This mound is 20' high and 170' × 100'-115' at the base. The ramp, about 10' wide, was centered on the west side of the mound, facing the large shell midden. The modern stairway is in the location of this original ramp. This mound and much of the site grounds are covered with a relatively dense growth of trees and shrubs.

DIRECTIONS: Near S shore of Terra Ceia Island, exit U. S. Route 19 onto Bayshore Dr., go W on Bayshore Dr. 1.5 mi. to site (Figure 66).

PUBLIC USE: Season and hours: Grounds are open 8:00 AM-Sunset, daily. **Fees:** None. **Restrictions:** Climbing on the platform mound, or disturbing or removing archeological features or objects, is prohibited. Pets must be on a 6' hand held leash. Intoxicants are not permitted on the site.

FOR ADDITIONAL INFORMATION: Contact: Manager, Gamble Plantation State Historic Site, 3708 Patten Avenue, Ellenton, FL 33532, 813-722-1017. **Read:** Bullen, Ripley P. 1951. The Terra Ceia Site, Manatee County, Florida. Florida Anthropological Society Publications no. 3.

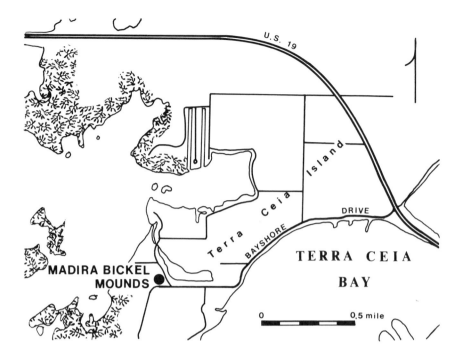

Figure 66. Location of Madira Bickel Mounds.

33. Arrowhead Park Middens

Mississippian Shell Middens
Pinellas County, Florida

Arrowhead Park middens, also known as the Mullet Key middens, are located at the north end of the west arm of Mullet Key in Arrowhead family picnic area, a large picnic facility within Fort Desoto Park. There are many middens in this area; most are no more than 3'-4' high and less than 15'-20' in diameter. The site dates from the Safety Harbor period.

These middens are not easily recognized for several reasons: (1) Many of these features are partly or completely obscured by the abundant loose sand. (2) Dredged or borrowed shell debris has been introduced to the site recently as road fill, thus increasing the amount of shell material that is visible. (3) The site was used as a gunnery and bombing range during World War II, so some areas contain recent explosive-generated "mounds" and "pits."

The middens, which can be recognized most easily by the concentration of bleached and brittle clam and oyster shells (unlike the more colorful and resilient recent shells), are most obvious between the entrance to Arrowhead Park and the point where the one-way loop begins (a distance of 0.1 mile). Entering the picnic area, watch for an open area to the left, just before the yellow and black "Caution Winding Road" sign on the right. Here the road crosses a large midden; it is low but obvious, and more easily recognized to the left (north) than to the right. At least two other middens occur between this large one and the barricaded service road on the right (southeast); one is at the service road and another is about 25' southwest of the service road.

On Tierra Verde Island is an historical marker commemorating Tierra Verde Mound, a Safety Harbor burial mound constructed about A.D. 1500. This marker is approximately 0.2 miles south of the southernmost (in 1987) condominium, along the east side of the Pinellas Bayway. Archeologists suspect that the same Indians built both the Tierra Verde Mound and the Arrowhead Park middens.

DIRECTIONS: From the southern end of Interstate Highway 275, or the intersection of U. S. Route 19 and 54th Avenue, in south St. Petersburg, go W on Florida State Route A19A (54th Ave. S/Pinellas Bayway) for 2.2 mi., then follow Pinellas Bayway S for about 7 mi. to Anderson Blvd. on Mullet Key, then go SW — then N — on Anderson Blvd. 3 mi. to Arrowhead family picnic area on right (Figure 67).

PUBLIC USE: Season and hours: The grounds are open daily, 7:00 AM-Sunset. **Fees:** None to enter park, but there is a $ .85 vehicle toll on the Pinellas Bayway. **Recreational facilities:** Picnic areas, restrooms, swimming, boating, camping, hiking, bicycling, birding. **Restrictions:** Disturbance of archeological sites or collection of archeological specimens in Pinellas County parks is strictly prohibited. Alcoholic beverages are not permitted in the park. Pets are allowed only in the picnic area, and must be on a 6′ (or shorter) leash. Ground fires are not permitted.

FOR ADDITIONAL INFORMATION: Contact: Pinellas County Park Department, 407 South Garden Ave., Clearwater, FL 33516, 813-462-3347.

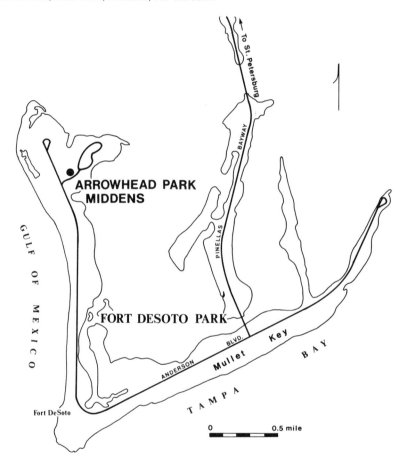

Figure 67. Location of Arrowhead Park Middens.

124

34. Bay Pines Mound

Late Archaic-Late Woodland Midden-Mound
Bay Pines, Pinellas County, Florida

A relatively large number of archeological sites existed in the Bay Pines area, but few of these have been studied and many have been destroyed as a result of intensive urbanization in Pinellas County. One archeological site in this area that has been studied is a combined midden and mound located on the grounds of the Bay Pines Veterans Administration Medical Center. The greater part of this feature is a shell midden which dates from the Late Archaic Period, perhaps some 4,000-2,500 years ago. Later, Timucuan or other Indians built a shallow burial mound on top of the midden sometime before A.D. 900. The combined midden and mound was about 5' high, 75' wide and 300' long; the midden was much more extensive than the mound.

Much of the Bay Pines midden and mound was excavated when a large part of the site was faced with destruction recently during construction of new facilities at the Medical Center. The southwestern end of this feature, however, remains in place and now abuts the patio of one of the Medical Center's nursing homes. This feature is grass covered, mown, and supports a few small trees; it can be seen easily from a paved road which passes within a few feet of the site. This mound is a small remnant of the original structure.

DIRECTIONS: Bay Pines V. A. Medical Center is located along the S side of U. S. Route Alternate 19 (Bay Pines Blvd.) in Bay Pines (Figure 68).

PUBLIC USE: Season and hours: Area is closed to the general public. Those with a special interest may see the mound by appointment only; for information contact Mr. Richard Van Alstine, Engineering Service, Building 17, 813-398-6661, extension 4587. **Restrictions:** Parking is not permitted in the vicinity of the mound. V.A.M.C. patients may not be photographed.

EDUCATIONAL FACILITIES: Interpretive exhibit: A small, informative display has been prepared by the Southeast Archaeological and Paleontological Society describing the archeology of the Bay Pines area and the Bay Pines Mound. A life size reconstruction of a Timucuan Indian is included. This display is on exhibit on the right (west) side of the lobby in the New Hospital (Building 100).

FOR ADDITIONAL INFORMATION: Read: Gallagher, John C., and Lyman O. Warren. 1972. Preliminary findings at the Bay Pines site. Bulletin, Tampa Bay Chapter, Florida Anthropological Society, vol. 4, no. 3, pp. 4-8.

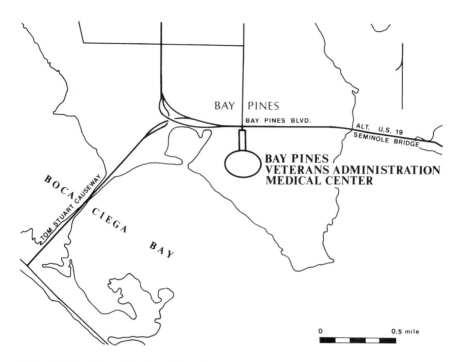

Figure 68. Location of Bay Pines Mound.

35. Safety Harbor Mound

Mississippian Platform Mound
Safety Harbor, Pinellas County, Florida

The Safety Harbor Site is located on Philippe Point, overlooking the west shore of Old Tampa Bay. This is a village site that was occupied by Tocobaga Indians between about A.D. 1500-1700. This could have been the political center of the Tocobaga Indians and the site that was visited by Pedro Menendez in 1567. This site is also the namesake of the Safety Harbor culture. Today, the site is located in Philippe Park, a Pinellas County facility named after Count Odet Philippe, a French immigrant who settled here in 1844, and who is credited with introducing the cultivation of grapefruit to the United States.

The Safety Harbor Site included a platform mound, a burial mound, a linear shell midden, and the associated village area, including possibly a plaza located west of the platform mound. Matthew W. Stirling first conducted test explorations of this site in 1929. The following year Stirling found more than 100 burials, along with many ceramic vessels that had been "killed" ceremonially, in the burial mound. (The bones uncovered by this excavation reportedly were taken by farmers and used as fertilizer.) The platform mound was investigated in 1948 by Ripley Bullen and John Griffin. Both mounds were found to have been built in stages — the burial mound primarily of sand and the platform mound of clay, sand, shell, and village debris.

Today only the platform mound is visible and interpreted. The feature has been subjected to shoreline erosion in the past, so a landscaped network of retaining walls and stairways has been built on the bay side of this mound. The mound is grass covered with several large trees growing upon it, and is clearly visible to observers.

DIRECTIONS: From U. S. Route 19, go E on Florida State Route 588 (Main St.) 2.5 mi. to Florida State Route 590 (Philippe Parkway), then N on Route 590 1.5 mi. to Philippe Park on E, then E into park 0.6 mi. to picnic shelter no. 2 parking area on E. Mound is behind shelter, toward Old Tampa Bay, and can be reached on foot from the picnic shelter parking area (Figure 69).

PUBLIC USE: Season and hours: Grounds are open daily, 7:00 AM-Sunset. **Fees:** None. **Recreational facilities:** Picnic areas, restrooms, walking, playgrounds, ball fields, bicycling. **Restrictions:** Disturbance of archeological sites or collection of archeological specimens in Pinellas County parks is strictly prohibited. Driving, or using bicycles, skates or skateboards on the paved ramp on the mound is prohibited. Dogs must be on a 6' (or shorter) leash. Alcoholic beverages are prohibited in park.

FOR ADDITIONAL INFORMATION: Contact: Pinellas County Park Department, 407 South Garden Ave., Clearwater, FL 33516, 813-462-3347. **Read:** Griffin, John W., and Ripley P. Bullen. 1950. The Safety Harbor Site, Pinellas County, Florida. Florida Anthropological Society Publications, no. 2.

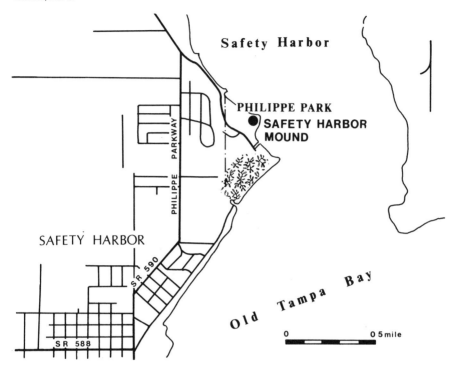

Figure 69. Location of Safety Harbor Mound.

36. Crystal River Mounds

Woodland and Mississippian Mound-Midden Complex
Citrus County, Florida

The Crystal River State Archaeological Site preserves, manages, and interprets one of the most significant publicly accessible prehistoric sites in Florida. The middens and mounds here span at least 1,600 years of human activity, from about 200 B.C. to A.D. 1400, and include features built by Woodland and Mississippian peoples. The site museum contains a large number of exhibits describing and interpreting the archeology of the site and region, and a well maintained system of asphalt trails leads throughout the midden and mound complex. Interpretive signs on the trail near the museum describe the Indian use of yaupon to make the *Black Drink* and coontie to make a staple flour. This site is well landscaped to permit easy viewing and comprehension of the archeological features; it is aesthetically pleasing and a pleasure to visit.

The earliest Indians that settled for any length of time (200 B.C.-A.D. 300) at Crystal River were those possessing Deptford and possibly Santa Rosa-Swift Creek cultural characteristics. Among other evidence of their presence, these early settlers started a burial mound built of sand upon an earthen platform and a shell midden. About A.D. 300, and for all or part of the next one thousand years, Weeden Island people inhabited the Crystal River site. A platform mound, built largely of shell and earth, might have been established around A.D. 600-700 adjacent to and over part of the village midden. In addition, a circular sand embankment up to 6' high was built for burials around the old, by then very crowded, burial mound. The Weeden Island people were followed by people of the Mississippian Safety Harbor culture, who occupied the site for about a century, from A.D. 1300-1400. During that period, a plaza was added to the village, and a second burial mound and a shell-and-earthen platform mound were built. The larger platform mound also might have been built by Safety Harbor people instead of the Woodland Weeden Island people.

The midden at Crystal River is long, narrow, and somewhat winding, with small mounded heaps located upon it at places. Some or all of these shell mounds were used as dwelling sites. (The Crystal River Site is barely above sea level today. The middens, in effect, created relatively high, and thus dry, ground — preferred sites for dwelling construction. This elevational effect can be seen clearly on the southwest side of the site, especially while descending the steps leading to the top of the larger temple mound. Although relative sea level was lower when the Indian settlement of Crystal River began than today, it has been rising for much of the last 2,000 or so years and would have been near its present level during the late Weeden Island and the Safety Harbor periods.)

The older burial mound is significant in that it has been the most intensively investigated feature at Crystal River. Clarence Moore first excavated this mound (and the flanking ridge) in 1903 and found more than 400 burials. Also recovered from this mound was a spectacular collection of artifacts (including mica sheets, copper ornaments, shell and stone objects) representing the Santa Rosa-Swift Creek culture that suggested strong connections with the contemporaneous Hopewell culture centered in the Ohio Valley. Yet another important aspect of the Crystal River Site is the presence of two crude stone stelae (ceremonial stones) — one of which is incised. These stelae were associated with the primitive solar calendar and observatory presumed to have existed here during Weeden Island or Safety Harbor time, and to some archeologists represent strong evidence for contact between the Indians of Crystal River and the Yucatan Peninsula, Mexico.

DIRECTIONS: From combined U. S. Routes 19/98 2 mi. N of Crystal River, go W 0.9 mi. on West State Park Street, then S 0.8 mi. on North Museum Point road to site entrance (Figure 70).

PUBLIC USE: Season and hours: Grounds are open 8:00 AM-Sunset, daily. **Fees:** None for admission to grounds. **Restrictions:** Pets must be on a 6' hand held leash and well behaved at all times. Pets are not allowed in the visitor center. Intoxicants are not permitted in the park.

EDUCATIONAL FACILITIES: Museums: The museum includes exhibits on a variety of archeological subjects. Emphasis is, of course, on the archeology of the Crystal River Site and environs; exhibits include a relief map of the site as it might have appeared about A.D. 1300, and descriptions and interpretations of the various cultures represented at the site, their technologies, trade networks, and use of natural resources. Other exhibits present information on archeological methods, cultural diffusion to and from the Crystal River region, and world cultures and cultural objects contemporaneous with the early occupation (ca. 150 B.C.-A.D. 100) of Crystal River. **Museum hours:** 9:00 AM-5:00 PM, Thursday through Monday. Closed Tuesday and Wednesday. **Fees:** Admission $.50; children 6 and under admitted free. **Trails:** Interpretive signs are located along trails throughout the site.

FOR ADDITIONAL INFORMATION: Contact: Manager, Crystal River State Archaeological Site, 3400 North Museum Pt., Crystal River, FL 32629, 904-795-3817. **Read:** (1) Moore, Clarence B. 1907. Crystal River revisited. Journal of the Academy of Natural Sciences of Philadelphia, vol. 13, pt. 3, pp. 406-425. (2) McMichael, Edward V. 1964. Veracruz, the Crystal River complex and the Hopewellian climax. Pp. 123-32 in J. R. Caldwell and R. L. Hall, (eds.), Hopewellian Studies, Illinois State Museum, Scientific Papers, vol. 12, no. 3.

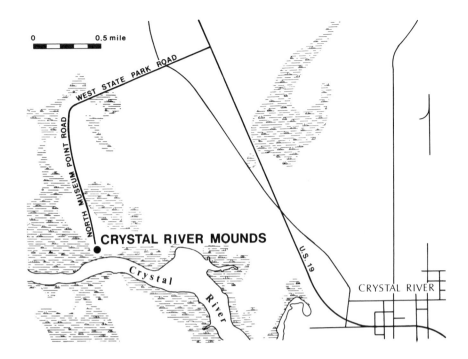

Figure 70. Location of Crystal River Mounds.

37. Shell Mound

Woodland Shell Midden
Levy County, Florida

Shell Mound is a large shell midden, primarily oyster with numerous clam and conch shells included, located along the mainland coast adjacent to Suwannee Sound. Several smaller middens also occur in the area. The main midden is about 12'-15' high and 1,500'-2,000' in circumference. A road formerly encircled the midden; half of this is now barricaded, but it is still possible to walk around the feature. A woodland dominated by live oak surrounds and covers the midden.

This midden is on the Lower Suwannee National Wildlife Refuge. The site is readily accessible but is not interpreted.

DIRECTIONS: From Florida State Route 24, about 19 mi. SW of combined U. S. Routes 19/98, go N on Levy County Road C347 2.5 mi., then W on Levy County Road C326 (the first paved road to the left) for 3.4 mi. Continue 0.12 mi. to woodland and small middens; Shell Mound is an additional 0.08 mi. ahead, on left (Figure 71).

PUBLIC USE: Season and hours: The refuge grounds are open 24 hours each day. **Fees:** None. **Recreational facilities:** Picnic area, restrooms, camping (0.1 mi. E of refuge boundary; county owned and maintained); boat landing and fishing on refuge. **Restrictions:** Vehicles are prohibited within the barricaded and posted areas. Camping and firearms are prohibited on refuge lands. Disturbing or removing archeological, plant, and animal resources is prohibited. Contact refuge manager for additional regulations.

FOR ADDITIONAL INFORMATION: Contact: U. S. Fish and Wildlife Serice, P. O. Box 851, Chiefland, FL 32626.

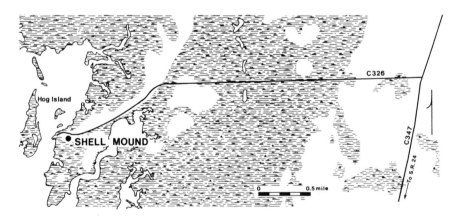

Figure 71. Location of Shell Mound.

38. Lake Lafayette Mound

Mississippian Platform Mound
Leon County, Florida

The Lake Lafayette Mound is a flat-topped pyramidal mound approximately 15' high. Ceramic artifacts collected from the vicinity of this feature indicate that a village surrounded the mound.

This mound lies about 100 yards south of Buck Lake Road on private property, directly opposite the entrance to a residential development located on the north side of Buck Lake road. The mound is nearly in line with the end of a log fence which parallels Buck Lake Road on the south for a short distance and serves as a landmark to help locate the mound. Large trees cover the mound, but it can be seen easily from Buck Lake Road across an open field.

DIRECTIONS: From combined U. S. Routes 90/319 intersection, go 0.9 mi. E on U. S. Route 90, then go SE 0.5 mi. on Buck Lake Road to mound on S side of road (Figure 72).

PUBLIC USE: Restrictions: Lake Lafayette Mound is on private property. Permission should be obtained from the land owner before entering upon the property.

FOR ADDITIONAL INFORMATION: Contact: Bureau of Archaeological Research, Division of Historical Resources, Department of State, Tallahassee, FL 32399-0250, 904-487-2299.

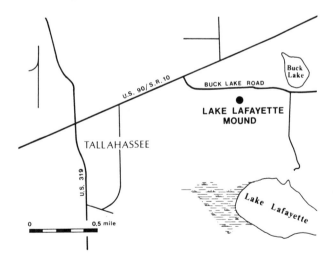

Figure 72. Location of Lake Lafayette Mound.

39. Velda Mound

Mississippian Platform Mound
Leon County, Florida

Velda Mound is an example of a single, relatively small platform mound such as would have been associated with a small permanent settlement that was a satellite of a larger Mississippian settlement and ceremonial center. The mound was probably about 8'-10' high when it was in use.

Velda Mound lies adjacent to a residential area. The site is fenced, but a walk-through gate permits access by pedestrians. This mound is overgrown with trees and is in a state of disrepair, but it was recently acquired by the State of Florida in order to afford this feature greater protection.

DIRECTIONS: From combined U. S. Route 319/Florida Route 61 (Thomasville Rd.), about 0.8 mi. N of intersection with Interstate Highway 10, go 1.1 mi. E on Killearney Way, then S 0.35 mi. on Raymond Diehl Rd., then E 0.35 mi. on Vassar Rd., then S 0.2 mi. on Riddle Dr., then E 0.05 mi. on Baldwin Dr. S to Velda Mound on S side of street (Figure 73).

FOR ADDITIONAL INFORMATION: Contact: Bureau of Archaeological Research, Division of Historical Resources, Department of State, Tallahassee, FL 32399-0250, 904-487-2299.

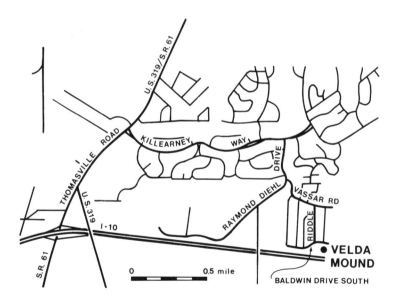

Figure 73. Location of Velda Mound.

40. Lake Jackson Mounds

Mississippian Ceremonial Center
Leon County, Florida

The Lake Jackson mounds comprise the most important and best preserved late Mississippian ceremonial center in western Florida and the largest known ceremonial center of the Fort Walton culture. These mounds were built during the late prehistoric period, probably between A. D. 1200 and 1500, on a swath of relatively level land between an arm of Lake Jackson on the east and rolling hills to the west. The site once contained at least six mounds, all apparently truncated pyramids, distributed over about 66 acres. The largest of the mounds is about 25' high and measures about 210' × 150' at the base; an earthen ramp might have been located on the east side of this mound. Religious and political leaders were buried in the floors of Mound C. Following each burial, the mound was restored, enlarged, and occupied by the next leader. The second largest mound is about 12' high and measures 110' × 140' at the base. Structures for religious and political leaders surmounted the mounds and overlooked the village plaza. Residences of the more ordinary people and planted fields probably surrounded the mound area. The cemetery would have been outside the village area. Smaller farming villages that were probably bound to the Lake Jackson ceremonial center by economic, religious and political ties existed at nearby locations, such as Lake Lafayette (see Lake Lafayette Mound).

Today, 41 acres of this mound complex and village area are incorporated in the Lake Jackson Mounds State Archaeological Site administered by the Florida Department of Natural Resources. Three of the mounds, including the two largest, are within the state-owned site. The two large mounds are connected by a foot trail that leads to the top of each. This site has been excavated on several occasions and is one of the better studied Mississippian sites in western Florida.

DIRECTIONS: From Interstate Highway 10, go N on combined U. S. Route 27/Florida State Route 63 1.8 mi., then E on Crowder Road 1.0 mi., then S on Indian Mound Road 0.5 mi. to Lake Jackson Mounds State Archaeological Site. From Florida State Route 157 southbound, go S on U. S. 27/Florida 63 2.7 mi. to Crowder Road, then continue as above (Figure 74).

PUBLIC USE: Season and hours: Open year round, 8:00 AM-Sunset. **Fees:** None. **Recreational facilities:** Picnic area, restrooms, foot trails. **Restrictions:** Climbing or walking on the sides of mounds except on steps provided, digging in mounds, and removing artifacts, plants or animals are prohibited. Pets must be on a hand held leash no greater than 6' in length. Intoxicants are not permitted on the site.

EDUCATIONAL FACILITIES: Trail: Interpretive signs are located along the trail to the mounds. The trail is about 0.1 mi. long (0.2 mi. round trip).

FOR ADDITIONAL INFORMATION: Contact: Ranger in Charge, Lake Jackson Mounds, State Archaeological Site, 1313 Crowder Road, Tallahassee, FL 32308, 904-562-0042. **Read:** Griffin, John W. 1950. Test excavations at the Lake Jackson Site. American Antiquity, vol. 16, pp. 99-112.

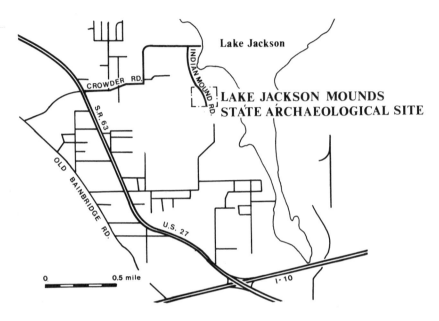

Figure 74. Location of Lake Jackson Mounds.

41. Chattahoochee Landing

Mississippian Ceremonial Center
Gadsden County, Florida

Chattahoochee Landing, located on the floodplain immediately east of the Apalachicola River, is one of the most important mound complexes known from along the Apalachicola River in Florida. Deptford ceramic shards have been found in one of the mounds, making this site one of the few that have yielded evidence of Early Woodland culture in the Apalachicola Valley. These ceramics could have been discarded by Deptford people in middens that were used later by Mississippian people to build their mounds. Alternatively, the ceramics could identify what is possibly a Deptford burial mound which the Mississippian people subsequently enlarged.

Most or all of the mounds date from the late Weeden Island-early Fort Walton time — about A.D. 800-1200. The major occupation of the site took place near the end of Weeden Island time. The site originally contained at least six, and possibly seven or more, earthen mounds. One of these was larger than the others, and appears to have been a truncated pyramid at least 11' high and measuring 170' × 100' at the base. All four of the other surviving mounds appear to have been circular; these vary now from about 2'-5' in height and from 45'-75' in diameter.

The five mounds that survive are located in a public park owned and maintained by the City of Chattahoochee as a boat landing on the Apalachicola River immediately south of U. S. Route 90. All of the mounds have been damaged to a greater or lesser degree. Erosion by flooding probably has done most damage to the site; perhaps half of the two largest remaining mounds have been lost to flood damage and one or more other mounds have apparently been obliterated entirely. Further damage has resulted from building and well construction during the 19th Century, excavation of the features, and indiscriminate motor vehicle traffic.

DIRECTIONS: From U. S. Route 90/Florida Route 269 intersection in Chattahoochee, follow Route 90 (W. Washington St.) W 0.3 mi., then go SW 0.3 mi. on River Landing Road to Chattahoochee Landing site. From E end of Route 90 bridge over Apalachicola River, go E 0.4 mi., then SW on River Landing Road to site (Figure 75).

PUBLIC USE: Season and hours: Open daily throughout the year.

FOR ADDITIONAL INFORMATION: Contact: City Superintendent, P. O. Drawer 188, Chattahoochee, FL 32324, 904-663-4475 *or* Bureau of Archaeological Research, Division of Historical Resources, Department of State, Tallahassee, FL 32399-0250, 904-487-2299. **Read:** Moore, Clarence B. 1903. Aboriginal mounds of the Apalachicola River. Journal of the Academy of Natural Sciences of Philadelphia, vol. 12, pp. 440-490.

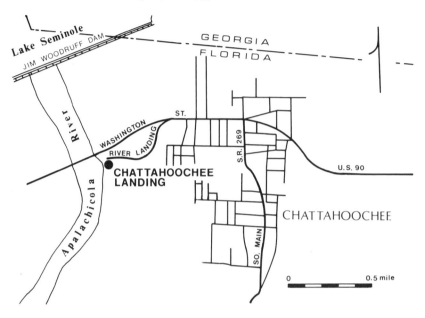

Figure 75. Location of Chattahoochee Landing Site.

42. Indian Temple Mound

Mississippian Platform Mound
Fort Walton Beach, Okaloosa County, Florida

Indian Temple Mound is located in a small park in Fort Walton Beach, Florida. This mound, and the adjacent Indian Temple Mound Museum, are owned and operated by the City of Fort Walton Beach. Stairs lead to the top of the mound where a representation of a Mississippian temple has been constructed. The sides and area around the base of the mound support many large trees. The park is lighted at night. Off-street parking is available on both the north and south side of the park.

Indian Temple Mound is the most conspicuous remnant of a much larger archeological site that appears to have been used more-or-less continuously from about 50 B.C.-A.D. 100 to about A.D. 1650 by a succession of Indian cultures. People possessing Deptford (50 B.C.-A.D.100), Santa Rosa-Swift Creek (A.D.100-500), Weeden Island (A.D. 500-1000), and Fort Walton (A.D. 1200-1650) cultural traits occupied the site. The Weeden Island culture is well represented in archeological collections from Fort Walton Beach, and has been interpreted as a period of prehistoric cultural climax for the northwest Florida Gulf Coast area (Figure 76). The construction of mounds specifically for burials were traits of the Deptford through Weeden Island cultures. Indian Temple Mound was built during Fort Walton time by agriculturalists who either migrated south or southeast from, or were influenced by cultures in, the Middle Mississippian culture region. Indian Temple Mound is somewhat unusual in that it was built near the Gulf Coast by the Fort Walton farming people where environmental conditions for agriculture were less favorable than at locations farther inland, where Fort Walton sites are typically located. One explanation for the success of this coastal farming center is that the shell from middens left by earlier occupants improved the soil quality to the extent that farming was viable. Available evidence indicates, however, that fishing and shellfishing were in fact more important at this site than farming.

Several excavations have been carried out at Indian Temple Mound and the surrounding area since 1883. At least three stages of mound construction have been documented, and more stages are possible since erosion and prior disturbance had removed some of the outer surface of the mound and the initial stage of construction has not been identified conclusively by excavators. More than 60 burials have been recovered from the mound. The mound could have been built as late as A.D. 1500-1650; it was nearly square (measuring about 12' high and 220' × 223' at the base) and had a ramp centered on its south side.

Figure 76. A funeral urn crafted by people of the Weeden Island culture. Fine ceramic crafts-manship, including the manufacture of effigy wares, was a characteristic of Weeden Island people. (Indian Temple Mound Museum photograph.)

DIRECTIONS: Follow U. S. Route 98 W 0.4 mi. from bridge over Santa Rosa Sound, or E 0.3 mi. from junction with Florida State Route 189 (Beal Parkway), to parking area in park off N side of Route 98. Alternatively, follow Florida State Route 85 S 1.6 mi. from bridge over Cinco Bayou, or N 0.1 mi. from junction with U. S. Route 98, to parking area in park off S side Florida 85. Street signs also provide directions to the mound and museum (Figure 77).

PUBLIC USE: Season and hours: Grounds are open 24 hours each day. **Fees:** None. **Restrictions:** Overnight camping or consumption of alcohol are prohibited.

EDUCATIONAL FACILITIES: Museum: The Indian Temple Mound Museum depicts 10,000 years of prehistory and early history of the northwestern Gulf Coast of Florida and environs. Exhibits describe and interpret technological, spiritual and artistic characteristics of seven Pre-Columbian Indian cultures. Also on exhibit are European artifacts representing the period of early contact between Europeans and Indians. Of special significance are the important collections of Weeden Island and Fort Walton ceramics housed at this museum. A "touch table" allows visitors the opportunity to handle and use replicas of tools used by area Indians, or to observe staff members demonstrating the use of these tools. Foreign language guide sheets are available for visitors. **Museum hours:** 11:00 AM-4:00 PM, Tuesday through Saturday; 1:00-4:00 PM, Sunday. Closed Monday, Thanksgiving, Christmas, New Years Day. **Fees:** Admission $.50. **Bookstore:** The museum shop offers for sale a wide selection of books on archeology, anthropology, southeastern Indian history and related subjects; reprints from *The Florida Anthropologist;* and other educational materials. The museum shop also sells books and reprints by mail. **Special group activities:** With prior arrangements, museum tours and special slide presentations are available for groups.

FOR ADDITIONAL INFORMATION: Contact: Curator, Indian Temple Mound Museum, P. O. Box 4009, Fort Walton Beach, FL 32549, 904-243-6521. **Read:** (1) Fairbanks, Charles H. 1965. Excavations at the Fort Walton Temple Mound, 1960. Florida Anthropologist, vol. 18, pp. 239-264. (2) Lazarus, Yulee W., and Robert J. Fornaro. 1975. Fort Walton Temple Mound (8OK6M): Further test excavations, De Pauw 1973. Florida Anthropologist, vol. 28, pp. 159-177.

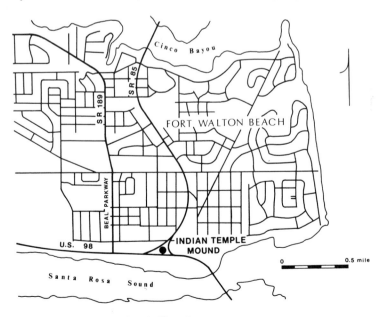

Figure 77. Location of Indian Temple Mound.

SECTION III

SOURCES OF ADDITIONAL INFORMATION

MUSEUM EXHIBITS

The following museums (in addition to those located at sites listed in Section II of this book) currently have exhibits that interpret the archeology of the mound- and midden-building Indians of the Atlantic Coast Region. These exhibits are normally parts of larger exhibits dealing with the archeology of the eastern United States or more localized regions, and therefore present the various cultures in their chronological and geographical context. These museums will provide group tours if such tours are requested well in advance of the tour date.

1. Historical Museum of Southern Florida. 101 W. Flagler St., Miami, FL 33130, 305-372-1492. Hours: Monday-Wednesday and Friday-Saturday, 10:00 AM-5:00 PM; Thursday, 10:00 AM-9:00 PM; Sunday, 12:00 Noon-5:00 PM. Closed New Years and Christmas.

2. Museum of Florida History, R. A. Gray Building, Bronough St., Tallahassee, FL 32399-0250, 904-488-1484. Hours: Monday through Friday, 9:00 AM-4:30 PM; Saturday, 10:00 AM-4:30 PM; Sunday and holidays, 12:00 Noon-4:30 PM. Closed Christmas.

3. Museum of the American Indian, Heye Foundation, Broadway at 155th St., New York, NY 10032, 212-283-2420. Hours: Tuesday through Saturday, 10:00 AM-5:00 PM; Sunday, 1:00-5:00 PM. Closed Monday and legal holidays.

4. South Carolina State Museum, 301 Gervais St., P. O. Box 100107, Columbia, SC 29202-3107, 803-737-4921. This museum is temporarily closed but is scheduled to reopen by the Fall of 1988. An exhibit on the prehistory of South Carolina will include information about the prehistoric use of shell mound and Mississippian platform mound sites.

5. The State Museum of Pennsylvania, Third and North Streets, Harrisburg, PA 17108-1026, 717-787-4978. Hours: Tuesday through Saturday, 9:00 AM-5:00 PM; Sunday, 12:00 Noon-5:00 PM. Closed Mondays and national holidays.

PUBLICATIONS

The books and articles listed here are representative of professional and popular publications available on the mound and midden building Indians of the Atlantic Coast Region. This list includes the most important publications of the 19th Century, at least one report for each site listed in Section II of this book (if such reports are available and reasonably substantive) and other significant mound and midden sites, and additional publications that present recent views on the archeology of the builders of the mounds and middens of the Atlantic Coast Region. The actual list of titles dealing with these Indians is extensive, but the publications listed here will introduce readers to the literature on the subject.

Historical Perspectives

Atwater, Caleb. 1820. "Description of the antiquities discovered in the state of Ohio and other western states." Archaeologia Americana: Transactions and Collections of the American Antiquarian Society, vol. 1, pp. 109-251.

Bartram, William. 1791. Travels through North and South Carolina, Georgia, East and West Florida, the Cherokee Country, the Extensive Territories of the Muscogulges, or Creek Confederacy, and the Country of the Chactaws. Philadelphia: James and Johnson.

Jefferson, Thomas. 1787 (1954). Notes on the State of Virginia. New York: W. W. Norton & Co. (W. Peden, ed.).

Jones, Charles C., Jr. 1873. Antiquities of the Southern Indians, Particularly of the Georgia Tribes. New York: D. Appleton and Co.

Mooney, James. 1900. Myths of the Cherokee. Bureau of American Ethnology, 19th Annual Report.

Morlot, A. 1861. "General views on archaeology." Annual Report of the Smithsonian Institution for 1860, pp. 284-343.

Squier, Ephraim G., and Edwin H. Davis. 1848. Ancient Monuments of the Mississippi Valley. Smithsonian Contributions to Knowledge 1.

Shetrone, Henry C. 1930. The Mound-Builders. New York: Appleton-Century.

Thomas, Cyrus. 1894. Report on the Mound Explorations of the Bureau of Ethnology. Washington, D.C.: Bureau of American Ethnology, Twelfth Annual Report, 1890-91. (This report was reprinted in 1985 by the Smithsonian Institution Press, with an introduction by Bruce D. Smith.)

Trigger, Bruce G., (ed.). 1986. Native Shell Mounds of North America: Early Studies. New York: Garland Publishing, Inc.

Vanuxem, Lardner. 1843. "On the ancient oyster shell deposits observed near the Atlantic coast of the United States." Reports of the first, second, and third meetings of the Association of American Geologists and Naturalists at Philadelphia, in 1840 and 1841, and at Boston in 1842, embracing its Proceedings and Transactions, pp. 21-23.

Willoughby, C. C. 1935. Antiquities of the New England Indians. Peabody Museum, Harvard University.

Wyman, Jeffries. 1875. Fresh-Water Shell Mounds of the St. John's River, Florida. Memoirs of the Peabody Academy of Science, Fourth Memoir.

Context and Overview

Bennett, Charles E. (Comp.). 1968. Settlement of Florida. Gainesville: University of Florida Press.

Bennett, John W. 1944. "Middle American influences on cultures of the southeastern United States." Acta Americana, vol. 2, pp. 25-50.

Bierer, Bert W. 1972. South Carolina Indian Lore. Columbia: Bert W. Bierer.

Bierer, Bert W. 1980. Indians and Artifacts in the Southeast. Columbia: Bierer Publishing Co.

Coe, Joffre L. 1964. The Formative Cultures of the Carolina Piedmont. Transactions of the American Philosophical Society, n.s., no. 54.

Coe, Michael, Dean Snow and Elizabeth Benson. 1986. Atlas of Ancient America. New York: Facts on File Publications.

Custer, Jay F. 1984. Delaware Prehistoric Archaeology: An Ecological Approach. Newark: University of Delaware Press.

dePratter, Chester. (Ed.) The Late Prehistoric Southeast: A Source Book. New York: Garland Publishing, Inc.

Griffin, James B. 1978. "Eastern United States." Pp. 51-70 in R. E. Taylor and Clement W. Meighan (eds.), Chronologies in New World Archaeology, New York: Academic Press.

Haviland, William A., and Marjory W. Power. 1984. The Original Vermonters: Native Inhabitants, Past and Present. Hanover: University Press of New England.

Hudson, Charles. 1976. The Southeastern Indians. Knoxville: The University of Tennessee Press.

Jennings, Jesse D. 1974. Prehistory of North America. New York: McGraw-Hill, 2nd Edition.

Luer, George M., and Marion M. Almy. 1981. "Temple mounds of the Tampa Bay area." Florida Anthropologist, vol. 34, pp. 127-156.

Mathis, Mark A., and Jeffrey J. Crow. (Eds.) 1983. The Prehistory of North Carolina: An Archaeological Symposium. Raleigh: North Carolina Division of Archives and History.

McManamon, Francis P. 1982. "Prehistoric land use on outer Cape Cod." Journal of Field Archaeology, vol. 9, pp. 1-21.

McManamon, Francis P. (Ed.) 1984. Chapters in the Archeology of Cape Cod. Boston: National Park Service. Two volumes.

McManamon, Francis P., and Christopher L. Borstel. 1982. The Archeology of Cape Cod National Seashore. Philadelphia: Eastern National Parks and Monument Association.

McMichael, Edward V. 1964. "Veracruz, the Crystal River Complex and the Hopewellian Climax." Pp. 123-132 in J. R. Caldwell and R. L. Hall, (eds.), Hopewellian Studies, Illinois State Museum, Scientific Papers, vol. 12, no. 3.

Milanich, Jerald T. 1985. The Early Prehistoric Southeast: A Source Book. New York: Garland Publishing, Inc.

Milanich, Jerald T., and Charles H. Fairbanks. 1980. Florida Archaeology. New York: Academic Press.

Milanich, Jerald T., and Samuel Proctor. (Eds.). 1978. Tacachale: Essays on the Indians of Florida and southeastern Georgia during the Historic Period. Gainesville: University Presses of Florida.

Morgan, William N. 1980. Prehistoric Architecture in the Eastern United States. Cambridge: MIT Press.

Ritchie, William A. 1980. The Archaeology of New York State. Harrison: Harbor Hill Books, Revised edition.

Silverberg, Robert. 1986. The Mound Builders. Athens: Ohio University Press.

Smith, Bruce D. 1985. "Introduction to the 1985 edition." Pp. 5-19 in Cyrus Thomas, Report on the Mound Explorations of the Bureau of Ethnology. Washington, D.C.: Smithsonian Institution Press. (Reprint of 1894 edition.)

Snow, Dean R. 1980. The Archaeology of New England. New York: Academic Press.

Spiess, Arthur E. 1985. "Wild Maine and the rusticating scientist: A history of anthropological archaeology in Maine." Man in the Northeast, no. 30, pp. 101-129.

Stuart, George E. 1972. "Mounds: Riddles from the Indian past." National Geographic Magazine, vol. 142, pp. 782-801.

Trigger, Bruce G. 1986. "Introduction." Pp. xi-xxiv in Bruce G. Trigger (ed.), Native Shell Mounds of North America: Early Studies. New York: Garland Publishing, Inc.

Waring, Antonio J., Jr., and Preston Holder. 1945. "A prehistoric ceremonial complex in the southeastern United States." American Anthropologist, vol. 47, pp. 1-34.

Wauchope, Robert. 1966. Archaeological Survey of Northern Georgia with a Test of some Cultural Hypotheses. Memoirs of the Society for American Archaeology, no. 21.

Willey, Gordon R. 1949. Archeology of the Florida Gulf Coast. Smithsonian Miscellaneous Collections, vol. 113.

Willey, Gordon R. 1966. An Introduction to American Archaeology, Volume 1: North and Middle America. Englewood Cliffs: Prentice Hall, Inc.

Willey, Gordon R., and Jeremy A. Sabloff. 1974. A History of American Archaeology. San Francisco: W. H. Freeman & Co.

Williams, Stephen. (Ed.). 1977. The Waring Papers: The Collected Works of Antonio J. Waring, Jr. Papers of the Peabody Museum of Archaeology and Ethnology, Harvard University, vol. 58. (Revised edition.)

Current Views

Bailey, G. N. 1983. "Problems of site formation and the interpretation of spatial and temporal discontinuities in the distribution of coastal middens." Pp. 559-582 in P. M. Masters and N. C. Fleming (eds.), Quaternary Coastlines and Marine Archaeology: Towards the Prehistory of Land Bridges and Continental Shelves. New York: Academic Press.

Barber, Russel. 1983. "Diversity in shell middens: The view from Morrill Point." Man in the Northeast, vol. 25, pp. 109-125.

Brennan, Louis A. 1977. "The midden is the message." Archaeology of Eastern North America, vol. 5, pp. 122-137.

Brose, David S. 1984. "Mississippian Period cultures in northwestern Florida." Pp. 165-197 in Dave D. Davis (ed.), Perspectives on Gulf Coast Prehistory. Gainesville: University of Florida Press.

Brose, David S., and N'omi Greber. 1979. Hopewell Archaeology: The Chillicothe Conference. Kent: The Kent State University Press.

Carr, Robert S. 1985. "Prehistoric circular earthworks in south Florida." Florida Anthropologist, vol. 38, pp 288-301.

Claassen, Cheryl. 1986. "Shellfishing seasons in the prehistoric southeastern United States." American Antiquity vol. 51, pp. 21-37.

Cumbaa, Stephen L. 1976. A reconsideration of freshwater shellfish exploitation in the Florida Archaic. Florida Anthropologist, vol. 29, pp. 49-59.

Ham, Leonard C., and Moira Irvine. 1975. "Techniques for determining seasonality of shell middens from marine mollusc remains." Syesis vol. 8, pp. 363-373.

Hudson, Charles M. 1979. Black Drink: A Native American Tea. Athens: University of Georgia Press.

Keel, B. C. 1976. Cherokee Archaeology: A Study of the Appalachian Summit. Knoxville: The University of Tennessee Press.

Killingley, J. S. 1981. "Seasonality of mollusc collecting determined from 0-18 profiles in midden shells." American Antiquity, vol. 46, pp. 152-158.

Kraft, J. C., D. F. Belknap, and I. Kayan. 1983. "Potentials of discovery of human occupation sites on the continental shelves and nearshore coastal zone." Pp. 87-120 in P. M. Masters and N. C. Fleming (eds.), Quaternary Coastlines and Marine Archaeology: Towards the Prehistory of Land Bridges and Continental Shelves. New York: Academic Press.

Larson, Lewis H. 1980. Aboriginal Subsistence Technology on the Southeastern Coastal Plain during the Prehistoric Period. Gainesville: University of Florida Press.

Milanich, Jerald T. 1980. "Weeden Island studies — past, present, and future." Southeastern Archaeological Conference Bulletin, vol. 22, pp. 11-18.

Muckle, Robert J. 1986. "Selected bibliography of molluscan archaeology." Zooarchaeological Research News, Supplement no. 3.

Sanger, David. 1981. "Unscrambling messages in the midden." Archaeology of Eastern North America, vol. 9, pp. 37-42.

Sears, William H. 1977. "Seaborne contacts between early cultures in lower southeastern United States and Middle through South America." Pp. 1-13 in Elizabeth P. Benson (ed.), The Sea in the Pre-Columbian World. Washington, D.C.: Dumbarton Oaks Research Library and Collections.

Seeman, Mark F. 1979. The Hopewell Interaction Sphere: The Evidence for Interregional Trade and Structural Complexity. Indiana Historical Society, Prehistory Research Series, vol. 5, no. 2.

Smith, Bruce D. (Ed.). 1978. Mississippian Settlement Patterns. New York: Academic Press.

Snow, Dean R. 1972. "Rising sea level and prehistoric cultural ecology in northern New England." American Antiquity, vol. 37, pp. 211-221.

Stoltman, James B., and David A. Baerreis. 1983. "The evolution of human ecosystems in the eastern United States." Pp. 252-268 in Herbert E. Wright, Jr. (ed.), Late-Quaternary Environments of the United States — Volume 2: The Holocene, Minneapolis: University of Minnesota Press.

Williamson, Ray A. (Ed.). 1981. Archaeoastronomy in the Americas. Los Altos: Ballena Press.

Site Reports:
Sites Identified in Section II

Broward County Archaeological Society and Miami-West India Archaeological Society, 1975. "The Arch Creek Site, Dade County." Florida Anthropologist, vol. 28, pp. 1-13.

Broyles, Bettye. J. 1964. (Abstract) "Mounds in Randolph County, West Virginia." Eastern States Archeological Federation Bulletin, vol. 23, p. 9. (Hyer Mound).

Bullen, Ripley P. 1951. "The Terra Ceia site, Manatee County, Florida." Florida Anthropological Society Publications no. 3.

Bullen, Ripley P. 1971. "The Sarasota County Mound, Englewood, Florida." Florida Anthropologist, vol. 24, no. 1, pp. 1-30.

Bullen, Ripley P., and Frederick W. Sleight. 1959. Archaeological Investigations of the Castle Windy Midden, Florida. William L. Bryant Foundation, American Studies Report 1.

Chadbourne, P. A. 1859. "Oyster Shell Deposit in Damariscotta." Collections of the Maine Historical Society, vol. 6, pp. 347-351.

Fairbanks, Charles H. 1946. "The Macon Earthlodge." American Antiquity, vol. 12, pp. 94-108.

Fairbanks, Charles H. 1965. "Excavations at the Fort Walton Temple Mound, 1960." Florida Anthropologist, vol. 18, pp. 239-264.

Fairbanks, Charles H., (with an introduction by Frank M. Setzler). 1980. Archeology of the Funeral Mound, Ocmulgee National Monument, Georgia. National Park Service, Archeological Research Series no. 3.

Gallagher, John C., and Lyman O. Warren. 1972. "Preliminary Findings at the Bay Pines Site." Bulletin, Tampa Bay Chapter, Florida Anthropological Society, vol. 4, no. 3, pp. 4-8.

Griffin, John W. 1950. "Test excavations at the Lake Jackson site." American Antiquity, vol. 16, pp. 99-112.

Griffin, John W., and Ripley P. Bullen. 1950. The Safety Harbor site, Pinellas County, Florida. Florida Anthropological Society Publications no. 2.

Heye, George G., F. W. Hodge, and George H. Pepper. 1918. The Nacoochee Mound in Georgia. Contributions, Museum of the American Indian, Heye Foundation, vol. 4, no. 3.

Kelly, Arthur R. 1938. A Preliminary Report on Archaeological Explorations at Macon, Georgia. Bureau of American Ethnology, Bulletin 119, Anthropological Papers, no. 1.

Laxson, Dan D. 1957. "The Arch Creek Site." Florida Anthropologist, vol. 10, nos. 3-4, pp. 1-13.

Lazarus, Yulee W., and Robert J. Fornaro. 1975. "Fort Walton Temple Mound (8OK6M): Further test excavations, De Pauw 1973." Florida Anthropologist, vol. 28, pp. 159-177.

Moore, Clarence B. 1894-96. "Certain sand mounds of the St. Johns River, Florida." Journal of the Academy of Natural Sciences of Philadelphia, vol. 10, nos. 1 and 2.

Moore, Clarence B. 1903. "Aboriginal mounds of Apalachicola River." Journal of the Academy of Natural Sciences of Philadelphia, vol. 12, pp. 4390-494. (Chattahoochee Landing site).

Moore, Clarence B. 1907. "Crystal River revisited." Journal of the Academy of Natural Sciences of Philadelphia, vol. 13, pt. 3, pp. 406-425.

Moorehead, Warren K. 1932. Etowah Papers. New Haven: Yale University Press.

Salwen, Bert. 1966. European Trade Goods and The Chronology of The Fort Shantok site. Archaeological Society of Connecticut, Bulletin 34, pp. 5-39.

Sanger, David, and Mary Jo (Elson) Sanger. 1986. "Boom and bust on the river: The story of the Damariscotta oyster shell heaps." Archaeology of Eastern North America, vol. 14, pp. 65-78.

Schell, Rolfe F. 1962. 1,000 Years on Mound Key. Fort Myers Beach: The Island Press.

Sears, William H. 1956. Excavations at Kolomoki, Final Report. University of Georgia Series in Anthropology, no. 5.

Simpkins, Daniel L. 1980. "A preliminary report on text excavations at the Sapelo Island Shell Ring, 1975." Pp. 61-75 in Daniel L. Juengst, (ed.), West Georgia College Studies in the Social Sciences, vol. 19.

South, Stanley. 1973. "The temple at Town Creek Mound State Historic Site, North Carolina." The Institute of Archeology and Anthropology — The University of South Carolina, Notebook, vol. 5, pp. 145-171.

Spiess, Arthur E., and Mark H. Hedden. 1983. Kidder Point and Sears Island in prehistory. Maine Historic Preservation Commission, Occasional Publications in Maine Archaeology, no. 3.

Waring, Antonio J., Jr., and Lewis H. Larson, Jr. 1977. "The shell ring on Sapelo Island." Pp. 263-278 in Stephen Williams, (ed.), The Waring Papers: The Collected Works of Antonio J. Waring, Jr. Papers of the Peabody Museum of Archaeology and Ethnology, Harvard University, vol. 58 (Revised edition.)

Site Reports:
Other Sites

Barber, Russell J. 1982. The Wheeler's Site, A Specialized Shellfish Processing Station on the Merrimack River. Peabody Museum of Archaeology and Ethnology, Harvard University, Peabody Museum Monographs, no. 7.

Bourque, Bruce J. 1975. "Comments on the Late Archaic populations of central Maine: The view from the Turner Farm." Arctic Anthropology, vol. 12, pp. 35-45.

Bullen, Ripley P. 1957. "The Barnhill Mound, Palm Beach County, Florida." Florida Anthropologist, vol. 10 (#1-2), pp. 23-36.

Bullen, Ripley P., and Frederick W. Sleight. 1960. Archaeological investigations of Green Mound, Florida. The William Bryant Foundation, American Studies, Report no. 2.

Caldwell, J. R., and Catherine McCann. 1941. Irene Mound Site, Chatham County, Georgia. Athens: University of Georgia Press.

Claflin, William H., Jr. 1931. Stalling's Island Mound, Columbia County, Georgia. Papers of the Peabody Museum of Archaeology and Ethnology, Harvard University, vol. 14, no. 1.

Coffin, Claude C. 1937. "A Prehistoric shell heap at the mouth of the Housatonic." Archaeological Society of Connecticut, Bulletin 5 (April), pp. 6-10.

Cushing, Frank H. 1897. "Exploration of ancient key-dweller remains on the Gulf Coast of Florida." Proceedings of the American Philosophical Society, vol. 25, no. 153, pp. 329-448.

Fewkes, Jesse W. 1924. "Preliminary archeological investigations at Weeden Island, Florida." Smithsonian Miscellaneous Collections, vol. 76, no. 13.

Gilliland, Marion S. 1975. The Material Culture of Key Marco, Florida. Gainesville: University Presses of Florida.

Goggin, John M., and Frank H. Sommer III. 1949. Excavations on Upper Matecumbe Key, Florida. Yale University Publications in Anthropology, no. 41.

Hadlock, W. S. 1939. The Tafts Point Shell Mound at West Gouldsboro, Maine. Robert Abbe Museum, Bulletin 5.

Hemmings, E. Thomas, and Kathleen A. Deagan. 1973. Excavations on Amelia Island in Northeast Florida. Contributions of the Florida State Museum, Anthropology and History 18.

Jahn, Otto L., and Ripley P. Bullen. 1978. The Tick Island site, St. Johns River, Florida. Florida Anthropological Society Publications 10.

Kellar, James H., A. R. Kelly, and E. V. McMichael. "The Mandeville site in southwest Georgia." American Antiquity, vol. 28, pp. 338-355.

Larson, Lewis H., Jr. 1957. "The Norman Mound, McIntosh County, Georgia." Florida Anthropologist, vol. 10, no. 1-2, pp. 37-52.

Matthew, G. F. 1884. "Discoveries at a village of the stone age at Bocabec, N. B." Bulletin of the Natural History Society of New Brunswick, vol. 3, pp. 6-29.

Moorehead, Warren K. 1912. Certain Peculiar Earthworks near Andover, Massachusetts. Department of Archaeology, Phillips Academy, Andover, Bulletin V.

Praus, A. A. 1942. "Excavation at the Old Lyme Shell Heap." Bulletin of the Archaeological Society of Connecticut, no. 13, pp. 3-66.

Rothschild, N. A., and L. Lavin. 1977. "The Kaeser Site: A stratified shell midden in the Bronx, New York." Bulletin of the New York State Archaeological Association, No. 70, pp. 1-27.

Schnell, Frank T., Vernon J. Knight, Jr., and Gail S. Schnell. 1981. Cemochechobee: Archaeology of a Mississippian Ceremonial Center on the Chattahoochee River. Gainesville: University of Florida Press.

Sears, William H. 1956. "The Turner River Site, Collier County, Florida." Florida Anthropologist, vol. 9, pp. 47-60.

Sears, William H. 1982. Fort Center: An Archaeological Site in the Lake Okeechobee Basin. Gainesville: University of Florida Press.

Sears, William H. 1967. "The Tierra Verde burial mound." Florida Anthropologist, vol. 20, pp. 25-73.

Sears, William H. 1971. "The Weeden Island site, St. Petersburg, Florida." Florida Anthropologist, vol. 24, pp. 51-60.

Setzler, Frank., and Jesse D. Jennings. 1941. The Peachtree Mound and Village Site, Cherokee County, North Carolina. Bureau of American Ethnology, Bulletin 131.

Smith, Ira F., III. 1973. "The Parker Site: A manifestation of the Wyoming Valley Culture." Pennsylvania Archeologist, vol. 43 (#3-4), pp. 1-53.

Speiss, Arthur E., Bruce J. Bourque and Steven L. Cox. 1983. "Cultural complexity in maritime cultures: Evidence from Penobscot Bay, Maine." Pp. 91-111 in Ronald J. Nash, (ed.), The Evolution of Maritime Cultures on the Northeast and the Northwest Coasts of America, Simon Fraser University, Department of Archaeology, Publication no. 11 (Turner Farm site).

Stephenson, R. L., and A. L. Ferguson. 1963. The Accokeek Creek Site: A Middle Atlantic Seaboard Culture Sequence. Museum of Anthropology, University of Michigan, Anthropological Papers, no. 20.

Protection and Management: Current Views

Ferguson, Leland. 1978. "Archaeology and cultural materials as a resource." Pp. 7-17 in Roy S. Dickens, Jr., and Carole E. Hill, (eds.). Cultural Resources: Planning and Management. Boulder: Westview Press.

Fitting, James E. 1982. "The status of rescue archeology in North America." Pp. 173-190 in Rex L. Wilson and Gloria Loyola, (eds.), Rescue Archeology: Papers from the First New World Conference on Rescue Archeology, Washington, D.C.: The Preservation Press.

King, T. F., P. P. Hickman and G. Berg. 1977. Anthropology in Historic Preservation: Caring for culture's clutter. New York: Academic Press.

McBryde, Isabel. (Ed.). 1985. Who Owns the Past? Melbourne, Victoria: Oxford University Press.

McGimsey, Charles R., III. 1972. Public Archeology. New York: Seminar Press.

Rolingson, Martha Ann. 1984. "Archaeology and prehistory in public parks, southeastern North America." Midcontinent Journal of Archaeology, vol. 9, pp. 155-171.

Maps of Mound and Midden Distribution

Billard, Jules B. (Ed.). 1974. The World of the American Indian. Washington, D.C.: The National Geographic Society, p. 64.

Coe, Michael, Dean Snow and Elizabeth Benson. 1986. Atlas of Ancient America. New York: Facts on File Publications, pp. 51, 54.

Shetrone, Henry C. 1930. The Mound-Builders. New York: Appleton-Century, figure 8.

Stuart, George E. 1972. "Mounds: Riddles from the Indian Past." National Geographic Magazine, vol. 142, pp. 782-801 (p. 791).

Thomas, Cyrus. 1894. Report on the Mound Explorations of the Bureau of Ethnology. Washington, D.C.: Bureau of American Ethnology, Twelfth Annual Report, 1890-91, plate XX.

Thomas, Cyrus. 1891. Catalogue of Prehistoric Works East of the Rocky Mountains. Bureau of American Ethnology, Bulletin 12, plate 1.

Other Relevant Publications

Bloom, Arthur L. 1983. "Sea level and coastal changes." Pp. 42-51 in Herbert E. Wright, Jr., (ed.), Late-Quaternary Environments of the United States — Volume 2: The Holocene, Minneapolis: University of Minnesota Press.

Gifford, George E., Jr. 1978. Dear Jeffie, being the letters from Jeffries Wyman, first director of the Peabody Museum, to his son, Jeffries Wyman, Jr. Cambridge: Peabody Museum Press.

Thoreau, Henry D. 1914. Cape Cod. Boston: Houghton Mifflin Co.

Wickliffe Mounds Research Center. 1986. Museum Directory: A Guide to Mississippian Indian Museum Sites, 1986. Wickliffe: Murray State University, Wickliffe Mounds Research Center.

TOPOGRAPHIC MAPS

Topographic maps show mound sites in their modern physical and cultural context. Listed below are the names of the topographic maps (quadrangles) upon which are located each of the sites described in Section II of this book. All or some of the mounds at the sites marked with an asterisk (*) are labeled on the respective maps; the locations of mounds at the other sites usually can be determined by reference to the location descriptions given in Section II. All maps named here are in the U. S. Geological Survey's 7.5 minute (7.5′, or 1:24,000 scale) series.

1. Kidder Point Site — Searsport, Maine
2. Damariscotta Middens — Damariscotta, Maine
3. Todd Site — Louds Island, Maine
4. Nauset Marsh Site — Orleans, Massachusetts
5. Fort Shantok — Uncasville, Connecticut
6. Romney Indian Mound — Romney, West Virginia
7. Hyer Mound — Valley Head, West Virginia
8. Town Creek Site* — Mount Gilead East, North Carolina
9. Nikwasi Mound* — Corbin Knob, North Carolina
10. Sewee Shell Ring — Bull Island, South Carolina
11. Spanish Mount* — Edisto Beach and Edisto Island, South Carolina
12. Sea Pines Shell Ring — Bluffton, South Carolina
13. Fort Watson Mound* — Saint Paul, South Carolina
14. Nacoochee Mound* — Helen, Georgia
15. Fort Mountain Stone Wall — Crandall, Georgia
16. Etowah Mounds* — Burnt Hickory Ridge and Cartersville, Georgia
17. Botanical Garden Mounds — Athens West, Georgia
18. Rock Eagle Effigy* — Rock Eagle Lake, Georgia
19. Ocmulgee Mounds* — Macon East, Georgia
20. Kolomoki Mounds* — Blakely North, Georgia
21. Sapelo Shell Ring — Sapelo Sound, Georgia
22. Canaveral Seashore Middens — Ariel, Florida
23. Mount Royal — Welaka, Florida
24. Alexander Springs Midden — Alexander Springs, Florida
25. Hontoon Island Midden — Orange City, Florida
26. Jupiter Inlet Lighthouse Midden — Jupiter, Florida
27. Jupiter Inlet Midden I — Jupiter, Florida
28. Arch Creek Midden — North Miami, Florida
29. Cutler Burial Mound — Perrine, Florida
30. Mound Key — Estero, Florida
31. Sarasota County Mound — Englewood, Florida
32. Madira Bickel Mounds —Palmetto, Florida
33. Arrowhead Park Middens — Pass-A-Grille Beach, Florida
34. Bay Pines Mound — Bay Pines, Florida
35. Safety Harbor Mound* — Oldsmar, Florida

36. Crystal River Mounds* — Red Level, Florida
37. Shell Mound* — Cedar Key, Florida
38. Lake Lafayette Mound — Lafayette, Florida
39. Velda Mound — Bradfordville, Florida
40. Lake Jackson Mounds — Lake Jackson and Tallahassee, Florida
41. Chattahoochee Landing Mounds — Chattahoochee, Florida- Georgia
42. Indian Temple Mound — Fort Walton Beach, Florida

Any of the topographic maps listed above may be purchased from: U. S. Geological Survey, Map Distribution, Federal Center, Building 41, Box 25286, Denver, Colorado 80225, 303-236-7477. Maps cost $2.50 each. There is a $1.00 handling charge if the total order is less than $10.00. Checks should be made payable to U. S. Geological Survey. Order by specifying name of quadrangle, state, and scale or series desired. All mail orders must be prepaid, including handling charges if necessary. Some maps are also available from various local private and government distributors.

INDEX

Mound Builders 45, 46
Mound Key 5, 56, 59, 117, 118
Mounds (burial) 12, 14, 15, 18, 27, 30, 31, 32, 35, 43, 44, 58, 59, 71, 72, 95, 98, 100, 102, 105, 115, 117, 121, 123, 125, 129, 130, 137, 139
Mounds (construction) 21, 29, 30, 31, 32, 34, 36, 127
Mounds (destruction) 34, 35, 47, 50, 51
Mounds (earthen) 23, 24, 29, 30, 58, 59
Mounds (platform) 1, 12, 20, 21, 24, 27, 31, 34, 35, 36, 50, 58, 59, 74, 76, 83, 85, 88, 98, 127, 129, 133, 134, 139
Mounds (shell) 23, 25
Mounds (stone) 23, 24, 28, 29, 58, 59, 91
Mount Royal 37, 56, 59, 105, 106
Mullet Key 50, 123
Museums 145

Nacoochee Mound 56, 57, 59, 84, 85
Nauset Marsh Site 47, 56, 58, 67, 68
New Brunswick 45
New England 6, 9, 10, 17, 30, 45
New England-Maritime Section 7, 8
New Jersey 2, 8
New York 1, 2, 9, 28, 30
Nikwasi Mound 37, 56, 58, 76, 77
North Carolina 1, 2, 13, 28, 37, 42, 44, 58, 74, 76

Ocmulgee National Monument 19, 33, 34, 35, 52, 56, 59, 95, 96, 97
Ohio 30, 44, 88
Ohio Hopewell Phase 5, 13, 15, 17, 18, 42, 130
Ohio River Valley 1, 5, 8, 13, 15, 41, 44, 46, 130

Paleo-Indian Period 10, 12, 14, 95
Paleo-Indian Tradition 12, 14
Pee Dee Phase 13, 19, 20, 74
Philadelphia 44, 46, 112
Philippe, Count Odet 127
Pickawaxent Creek 24, 48
Piedmont 7, 8, 93
Pile dweller sites 26
Pisgah Phase 13, 19, 20
Plaza (ceremonial) 21, 36, 74, 88
Potomac River 70, 71
Pottery 15, 21, 85, 100, 137
Poverty Point Phase 13
Powell, John Wesley 46
Protective legislation 51, 52, 53, 54, 57
Putnam, Frederic Ward 65

Qualla Phase 13, 76
Quaternary 8
Quebec 14

Raised fields 21, 36
Rock Eagle Effigy Mound 29, 56, 59, 93, 94
Romney Indian Mound 31, 56, 58, 70, 71